KARL MARX

His Life and Environment

ISAIAH BERLIN

A GALAXY BOOK

NEW YORK OXFORD UNIVERSITY PRESS 1959

First Published, 1939
Second Edition, 1948

First Published as a Galaxy Book, 1959

Printed in the United States of America

TO MY PARENTS

PREFATORY NOTE

My thanks are due to my friends and colleagues who have been good enough to read this book in manuscript, and have contributed valuable suggestions, by which I have greatly profited; in particular to Mr. A. J. Ayer, Mr. Ian Bowen, Mr. G. E. F. Chilver, Mr. S. N. Hampshire and Mr. S. Rachmilewitch; I am further greatly indebted to Mr. Francis Graham-Harrison for compiling the index; to Mrs. H. A. L. Fisher and Mr. David Stephens for reading the proofs; to Messrs. Methuen for permission to make use of the passage quoted on page 180; and, most of all, to the Warden and Fellows of All Souls College for permitting me to devote a part of the time during which I held a Fellowship of the college to a subject outside the scope of my proper studies.

I. B.

OXFORD
May 1939

CONTENTS

CHAPTER I

INTRODUCTION

> Things and actions are what they are, and their conse-
> quences will be what they will be: why then should we seek
> to be deceived?
>
> BISHOP BUTLER

No thinker in the nineteenth century has had so direct,
deliberate and powerful an influence upon mankind as
Karl Marx. Both during his lifetime and after it he
exercised an intellectual and moral ascendancy over his
followers, the strength of which was unique even in that
golden age of democratic nationalism, an age which saw
the rise of great popular heroes and martyrs, romantic,
almost legendary figures, whose lives and words dominated the imagination of the masses and created a
new revolutionary tradition in Europe. Yet Marx could
not, at any time, be called a popular figure in the ordinary sense: certainly he was in no sense a popular
writer or orator. He wrote extensively, but his works
were not, during his lifetime, read widely; and when,
in the late 'seventies, they began to reach the immense
public which several among them afterwards obtained,
the desire to read them was due not so much to a
recognition of their intrinsic qualities as to the growth
of the fame and notoriety of the movement with which
he was identified.

Marx totally lacked the qualities of a great popular
leader or agitator, was not a publicist of genius like the
Russian democrat Alexander Herzen, nor did he possess
Bakunin's marvellous eloquence; the greater part of
his working life was spent in comparative obscurity in

London, at his writing-desk and in the reading-room of the British Museum. He was little known to the general public, and while towards the end of his life he became the recognized, and admired, leader of a powerful international movement, nothing in his life or character stirred the imagination or evoked the boundless devotion, the intense, almost religious, worship, with which such men as Kossuth, Mazzini, and even Lassalle in his last years, were regarded by their followers.

His public appearances were neither frequent nor notably successful. On the few occasions on which he addressed banquets or public meetings, his speeches were overloaded with matter, and delivered with a combination of monotony and brusqueness, which commanded the respect but not the enthusiasm of his audience. He was by temperament a theorist and an intellectual, and instinctively avoided direct contact with the masses, to the study of whose interests his entire life was devoted. To many of his followers he appeared in the role of a dogmatic and sententious German schoolmaster, prepared to repeat his theses indefinitely, with rising sharpness, until their essence became irremovably lodged in his disciples' minds. The greater part of his economic teaching was given its first expression in lectures to working men: his exposition under these circumstances was by all accounts a model of lucidity and conciseness. But he wrote slowly and painfully, as sometimes happens with rapid and fertile thinkers, scarcely able to cope with the speed of their own ideas, impatient at once to communicate a new doctrine, and to forestall every possible objection; the published versions were generally turgid, clumsy, and obscure in detail, although the central doctrine is never in serious doubt. He was acutely conscious of this, and once compared himself with the hero of Balzac's *Unknown Masterpiece*, who tries to paint the picture which has formed itself in his mind, touches and retouches the canvas endlessly, to produce at last a shapeless mass of colours, which to his eye seems to express the vision in his imagination. He belonged to a generation which cultivated the emotions more intensely and deliberately than its predecessors, and was brought up among men to whom ideas were often more real than facts, and personal relations meant far more than the events of the external world; by whom indeed public life was commonly understood and interpreted in terms of the rich and elaborate world of their own private experience. Marx was by nature not introspective, and took little interest in persons or states of mind or soul; the failure on the part of so many of his contemporaries to assess the importance of the revolutionary transformation of the society of their day, due to the swift advance of technology with its accompaniment of sudden increase of wealth, and, at the same time, of social and cultural dislocation and confusion, merely excited his anger and contempt.

He was endowed with a powerful, active, unsentimental mind, an acute sense of injustice, and exceptionally little sensibility, and was repelled as much by the rhetoric and emotionalism of the intellectuals as by the stupidity and complacency of the bourgeoisie; the first seemed to him aimless chatter, remote from reality and, whether sincere or false, equally irritating; the second at once hypocritical and self-deceived, blinded to the salient features of its time by absorption in the pursuit of wealth and social status.

This sense of living in a hostile and vulgar world, intensified perhaps by his dislike of the fact that he was born a Jew, increased his natural harshness and aggressiveness, and produced the formidable figure of popular imagination. His greatest admirers would find it difficult to maintain that he was a sensitive or tender-hearted man, or in any way concerned about the feelings of those with whom he came into contact; the majority of the men he met were, in his opinion, either fools or sycophants, and towards such he behaved with open suspicion or contempt. But if his attitude in public was overbearing and offensive, in the intimate circle composed of his family and his friends, in which he felt completely secure, he was considerate and gentle; his married life was exceptionally happy, he was warmly attached to his children, and he treated his lifelong friend and collaborator, Engels, with uniform loyalty and devotion. He was a charmless man, and his behaviour was often boorish, but even his enemies were fascinated by the strength and vehemence of his personality, the boldness of his views, and the breadth and brilliance of his analyses of the contemporary situation.

He remained all his life an oddly isolated figure among the revolutionaries of his time, equally hostile to their persons, their methods and their ends. His isolation was not, however, due merely to temperament or to the accident of time and place. However widely the majority of European democrats differed in character, aims and historical environment, they resembled each other in one fundamental attribute, which made co-operation between them possible, at least in principle. Whether or not they believed in violent revolution, the great majority of them were, in the last analysis, liberal reformers, and appealed explicitly to moral standards common to all mankind. They criticized and condemned the existing condition of humanity in terms of some preconceived ideal, some system, whose desirability at least needed no demonstration, being self-evident to all men with normal moral vision; their schemes differed in the degree to which they could be realized in practice, and could accordingly be classified as less or more utopian, but broad agreement existed between all schools of democratic thought about the ultimate ends to be pursued. They disagreed about the effectiveness of the proposed means, about the extent to which compromise with the existing powers was morally or practically advisable, about the character and value of specific social institutions, and consequently about the policy to be adopted with regard to them. But they were essentially reformers in the sense that they believed that there was little which could not be altered by the determined will of individuals; they believed, too, that powerfully held moral ends were sufficient springs of action, themselves justified by an appeal not to facts but to some universally accepted scale of values. It followed that it was proper first to ascertain what one wished the world to be: next, one had to consider in the light of this how much of the existing social fabric should be retained, how much condemned: finally, one was obliged to look for the most effective means of accomplishing the necessary transformation.

With this attitude, common to the vast majority of revolutionaries and reformers at all times, Marx came to be wholly out of sympathy. He was convinced that human history is governed by laws which, like the laws which govern nature, cannot be altered by the intervention of individuals actuated by this or that ideal. He believed, indeed, that the inner experience to which men appeal to justify their ends, so far from revealing a special kind of truth called moral or religious, is merely a faculty which engenders myths and illusions, both individual and collective. Being conditioned by the material circumstances in which they come to birth, the myths embody in the guise of objective truth whatever men in their misery wish to believe; under their treacherous influence men misinterpret the nature of the world in which they live, misunderstand their own position in it, and therefore miscalculate the range of their own and others' power, and the consequences both of their own and their opponents' acts. In opposition to the majority of the democratic theorists of his time, Marx believed that values could not be contemplated in isolation from facts, but necessarily depended upon the manner in which the facts were viewed. True insight into the nature and laws of the historical process will of itself, without the aid of independently known moral standards, make clear to a rational being what step it is proper for him to adopt, that is, what course would most accord with the requirements of the order to which he belongs. Consequently Marx had no new ethical or social ideal to press upon mankind; he did not plead for a change of heart; a change of heart was necessarily but the substitution of one set of illusions for another. He differed from the other great ideologists of his generation by making his appeal, at least in his own view, solely to reason, to the practical intelligence, denouncing only intellectual vice or blindness, insisting that all that men need, in order to know how to save themselves from the chaos in which they are involved, is to seek to understand their actual condition; believing that a correct estimate of the precise balance of forces in the society to which men belong will itself indicate the form of life which it is rational to pursue. Marx denounces the existing order by appealing not to ideals but to history: he denounces it not as bad, or unfortunate, or due to human wickedness or folly, but as being caused by the laws of social development, which make it inevitable that at a certain stage of history one class should dispossess and exploit another. The oppressors are threatened not with deliberate retribution on the part of their victims, but with the inevitable destruction which history has in store for them, as a class doomed shortly to disappear from the stage of history.

Yet, designed though it is to appeal to the intellect, his language is that of a herald and a prophet, speaking in the name not of human beings but of the universal law itself, seeking not to rescue nor to improve, but to warn and to condemn, to reveal the truth, and above all to refute falsehood. *Destruam et ædificabo* ('I shall destroy and I shall build'), which Proudhon placed at the head of one of his works, far more aptly describes Marx's conception of his own appointed task. In 1845 he had completed the first stage of his programme, and acquainted himself with the nature, history and laws of the evolution of the society in which he found himself. He concluded that the history of society is the history of struggles of opposed classes, one of which must emerge triumphant, although in a much altered form: progress is constituted by the succession of victories of one class over the other, and that man alone is rational who identifies himself with the progressive class in his society, either, if need be, by deliberately abandoning his past and allying himself with it, or if history has already placed him there, by consciously recognizing his situation and acting in the light of it.

Accordingly Marx, having identified the rising class in the struggle of his own time with the proletariat, devoted the rest of his life to planning a victory for those at whose head he had placed himself. This victory the process of history would in any case secure, but human courage, determination and ingenuity could bring it nearer and make the transition less painful, accompanied by less friction and less waste of human substance. His position henceforth is that of a commander, actually engaged in a campaign, who therefore does not continually call upon himself and others to show reason for engaging in a war at all, or for being on one side of it rather than the other: the state of war and one's own position in it are given; they are facts not to be questioned but accepted and examined; one's sole business is to defeat the enemy; all other problems are academic, based on unrealized hypothetical conditions, and so beside the point. Hence the almost complete absence in Marx's later works of discussions of ultimate principles, of all attempts to justify his opposition to the bourgeoisie. The merits or defects of the enemy, or what might have been, if no enemy and no war existed, is of no interest during the battle. To introduce these irrelevant issues during the period of actual fighting is to divert the attention of one's supporters from the crucial issues with which, whether or not they recognize them, they are faced, and so to weaken their power of resistance.

All that is important during the actual war is accurate knowledge of one's own resources and of those of the adversary, and knowledge of the previous history of society and the laws which govern it is indispensable to this end. *Das Kapital* is an attempt to provide such an analysis. The almost complete absence from it of explicit moral argument, of appeals to conscience or to principle, and the equally striking absence of detailed prediction of what will or should happen after the victory, follow from the concentration of attention on the practical problems of action. The conceptions of natural rights, and of conscience, as belonging to every man irrespective of his position in the class struggle, are rejected as liberal illusions: socialism does not appeal, it demands; it speaks not of rights, but of the new form of life before whose inexorable approach the old social structure has visibly begun to disintegrate. Moral, political, economic conceptions and ideals alter no less than the social conditions from which they spring: to regard any one of them as universal and immutable is tantamount to believing that the order to which they belong—in this case the bourgeois order—is eternal. This fallacy underlies the ethical and psychological doctrines of idealistic humanitarians from the eighteenth century onwards. Hence the contempt and loathing poured by Marx upon the common assumption, made by liberals and utilitarians, that since the interests of all men are ultimately and have always been the same, a measure of goodwill and benevolence on the part of everyone may yet make it possible to manufacture some sort of general compromise. If the war is real, these interests are totally incompatible. A denial of this fact can be due only to stupid or cynical disregard of the truth, a peculiarly vicious form of hypocrisy or self-deception, repeatedly exposed by history. This fundamental difference of outlook, and no mere dissimilarity of temperament or natural gifts, is the property which distinguishes Marx sharply from the bourgeois radicals and utopian socialists whom, to their own bewildered indignation, he fought and abused savagely and unremittingly for more than forty years.

He detested romanticism, emotionalism, and humanitarianism of every kind, and, in his anxiety to avoid any appeal to the idealistic feelings of his audience, systematically removed every trace of the old democratic vocabulary from the propagandist literature of his movement. He neither offered nor invited concessions at any time, and did not enter into any dubious political alliances, since he declined all forms of compromise. The manuscripts of the numerous manifestoes, professions of faith and programmes of action to which he appended his name, still bear the strokes of the pen and the fierce marginal comments, with which he sought to obliterate all references to eternal justice, the equality of man, the rights of individuals or nations, the liberty of conscience, the fight for civilization, and other such phrases which were the stock in trade (and had once genuinely embodied the ideals) of the democratic movements of his time; he looked upon these as so much worthless cant, indicating confusion of thought and ineffectiveness in action.

The war must be fought on every front, and, since contemporary society is politically organized, a political party must be formed out of those elements which in accordance with the laws of historical development are destined to emerge as the conquering class. They must ceaselessly be taught that what seems so secure in existing society is, in reality, doomed to swift extinction, a fact which men may find it difficult to believe because of the immense protective façade of moral, religious, political and economic assumptions and beliefs, which the moribund class consciously or unconsciously creates, blinding itself and others to its own approaching fate. It requires both intellectual courage and acuteness of vision to penetrate this smoke-screen and perceive the real structure of events. The spectacle of chaos, and the imminence of the crisis in which it is bound to end, will of itself convince a clear-eyed and interested observer—for no one who is not virtually dead or dying, can be a disinterested spectator of the fate of the society with which his own life is bound up—of what he must be and do in order to survive. Not a subjective scale of values revealed differently to different men, determined by the light of an inner vision, but knowledge of the facts themselves, must, according to Marx, determine rational behaviour. The society which is judged to be progressive, and so worthy of support, is that which is capable of further expansion in its initial direction without an alteration of its entire basis. A society is reactionary when it is inevitably moving into an impasse, unable to avoid internal chaos and ultimate collapse in spite of the most desperate efforts to survive, efforts which themselves create irrational faith in its own ultimate stability, the anodyne with which all dying institutions necessarily delude themselves. Nevertheless, what history—to Marx an almost active agency—has condemned will be inevitably swept away: to say that it ought to be saved, even when that is not possible, is to deny the rational plan of the universe. To criticize the facts themselves was for Marx a form of childish subjectivism, due to a morbid or shallow view of life, to some irrational prejudice in favour of this or that virtue or institution; it revealed attachment to the old world and was a symptom of incomplete emancipation from its values. It seemed to him that under the guise of earnest philanthropic feeling there throve, undetected, seeds of weakness and treachery, due to a fundamental desire to come to terms with the reaction, a secret horror of revolution based on fear of the truth, of the full light of day. With the truth there could, however, be no compromise: and humanitarianism was but a softened, face-saving form of compromise, due to a desire to avoid the perils of an open fight and, even more, the risks and responsibilities of victory. Nothing stirred his indignation so much as cowardice: hence the furious and often brutal tone with which he refers to it, the beginning of that harsh 'materialist' style which struck an entirely unfamiliar note in the literature of revolutionary socialism. This fashion for 'naked objectivity' took the form, particularly among Russian writers of a later generation, of searching for the sharpest, most unadorned, most shocking form of statement in which to clothe what were sometimes not very startling propositions.

Marx had, by his own account, begun to build his new instrument from almost casual beginnings: because, in the course of a controversy with the Government on an economic question of purely local importance, in which he was involved in his capacity as editor of a radical newspaper, he became aware of his almost total ignorance of the history and principles of economic development. This controversy occurred in 1843. By 1848 his education as a political and economic thinker was complete. With prodigious thoroughness he had constructed a complete theory of society and its evolution, which indicated with absolute precision where and how the answers to all such questions must be sought and found. Its originality has often been questioned. It is original, not indeed in the sense in which works of art are original, when they embody some hitherto unexpressed individual experience, but as scientific theories are said to be original, when they provide a new solution to a hitherto unsolved problem, which they may do by modifying and combining existing views to form a new hypothesis. Marx never attempted to deny his debt to other thinkers: 'I am performing an act of historical justice, and am rendering to each man his due', he loftily declared. But he did claim to have provided for the first time a wholly adequate answer to questions which had been previously either misunderstood, or answered wrongly or insufficiently or obscurely. The characteristic for which Marx sought was not novelty but truth, and when he found it in the works of others, he endeavoured, at any rate during the early years in Paris, in which his thought took its final shape, to incorporate it in his new synthesis. What is original in the result is not any one component element, but the central hypothesis by which each is connected with the others, so that the parts are made to appear to follow from each other and to support each other in a single systematic whole.

To trace the direct source of any single doctrine advanced by Marx is, therefore, a relatively simple task which his numerous critics have been only too anxious to perform. It may well be that there is not one among his views whose embryo cannot be found in some previous or contemporary writer. Thus the doctrine of communal ownership founded upon the abolition of private property, has probably, in one or other form, possessed adherents at most periods during the last two thousand years. Consequently the often debated question whether Marx derived it directly from the writings of Mably, or from some German account of French Communism, is too purely academic to be of great importance. As for the more specific doctrines, historical materialism of a sort is to be found fully developed in a treatise by Holbach printed a century before, which in its turn owes much to Spinoza; a modified form of it was restated in Marx's own day by Feuerbach. The view of human history as the history of war between social classes is to be found in Saint-Simon, and was to a large extent adopted by such contemporary liberal French historians as Thierry and Mignet, and equally by the more conservative Guizot. The scientific theory of the inevitability of the regular recurrence of economic crises was probably first formulated by Sismondi; that of the rise of the Fourth Estate was certainly held by the early communists, popularized in Germany in Marx's own day by von Stein and Hess. The dictatorship of the proletariat was adumbrated by Babeuf in the last decade of the eighteenth century, and was explicitly developed in the nineteenth in different fashions by Weitling and Blanqui; the present and future position and importance of workers in an industrial state was more fully worked out by Louis Blanc and the French State Socialists than Marx is prepared to admit. The labour theory of value derives from Locke, Adam Smith and the classical economists; the theory of exploitation and surplus value, and of its remedy by deliberate State control, is found both in Fourier, and in the writings of early English socialists, such as Bray, Thompson and Hodgskin; the list could easily be continued further.

There was no dearth of such doctrines particularly in the eighteenth century. Some died at birth, others, when the intellectual climate was favourable, modified opinion and influenced action. Marx sifted this immense mass of chaotic material and detached from it whatever seemed to him original, true and important; and in the light of it constructed a new instrument of social analysis, the main merit of which lies not in its beauty or consistency, nor in its emotional or intellectual power—the great utopian systems are nobler works of the speculative imagination—but in the remarkable combination of simple fundamental principles with comprehensiveness, realism and detail. The environment which it assumed actually corresponded to the personal, first-hand experience of the public to which it was addressed; its analyses, when stated in their simplest form, seemed at once novel and penetrating, and the new hypotheses which represent a peculiar synthesis of German idealism, French rationalism, and English political economy, seemed genuinely to co-ordinate and account for a mass of social phenomena hitherto thought of in comparative isolation from each other. This provided a concrete meaning for the formulae and popular slogans of the new communist movement. Above all, it enabled it to do more than stimulate general emotions of discontent and rebellion by attaching to them, as Chartism had done, a collection of specific but loosely connected political and economic ends. It directed these feelings to systematically inter-connected, immediate, feasible objectives, regarded not as ultimate ends valid for all men at all times, but as objectives proper to a revolutionary party representing a specific stage of social development.

To have given clear and unified answers in familiar empirical terms to those theoretical questions which most occupied men's minds at this time, and to have deduced from them direct practical consequences with-out creating obviously artificial links between the two, was the principal achievement of Marx's theory, and endowed it with that singular vitality which enabled it to defeat and survive its rivals in the succeeding decades. It was composed largely in Paris during the troubled years between 1843 and 1850, when, under the stress of a world crisis, economic and political tendencies normally concealed below the surface of social life, increased in scope and in intensity until they broke through the framework which was secured in normal times by established institutions; and for a brief instant revealed their real character during the luminous interlude which preceded the final clash of forces in which all issues were obscured once more. Marx fully profited by this rare opportunity for scientific observation in the field of social theory; to him, indeed, it appeared to provide full confirmation of his hypotheses.

The system as it finally emerged was a massive structure, heavily fortified against attack at every strategic point, incapable of being taken by direct assault, containing within its walls elaborate resources to meet every conceivable contingency of war. Its influence has been immense on friend and foe alike, and in particular on social scientists, historians and critics. It has altered the history of human thought in the sense that after it certain things could never again be plausibly said. No subject loses, at least in the long run, by becoming a field of battle, and the Marxist emphasis upon the primacy of economic factors in determining human behaviour led directly to an intensified study of economic history, which, although it had not been entirely neglected in the past, did not attain to its present prominent rank, until the rise of Marxism gave an impulse to exact historical scholarship in that sphere—much as in the previous generation Hegelian doctrines acted as a powerful stimulus to historical studies in general. The sociological treatment of historical problems which Comte, and after him, Spencer and Taine, had discussed and mapped, became a precise and concrete study only when the attack of militant Marxism made its conclusions a burning issue, and so made the search for evidence more zealous and the attention to method more intense.

In 1849 Marx was forced to leave Paris, and came to live in England. Life in that country hardly affected him at all. To him London meant little more than the library of the British Museum, 'the ideal strategic vantage point for the student of bourgeois society', an arsenal of ammunition whose importance its owners did not appear to grasp. He remained almost totally unaffected by his surroundings, living encased in his own, largely German, world, formed by his family and a small group of intimate friends and political associates. He met few Englishmen and neither understood nor cared for them or their mode of life. He was a man unusually impervious to the influence of environment: he saw little that was not printed in newspapers or books, and remained until his death comparatively unaware of the quality of the life around him or of its social and natural background. So far as his intellectual development is concerned, he might just as well have spent his exile on Madagascar, provided that a regular supply of books and journals could have been secured: certainly the inhabitants of London could hardly have taken less notice of his existence if he had. The formative, psychologically most interesting, years of his life were over by 1849: after this he was emotionally and intellectually set and hardly changed at all. He had, while still in Paris, conceived the idea of providing a complete account and explanation of the rise and imminent fall of the capitalist system. His work upon it was begun in the spring of 1850, and continued, with interruptions, caused by day-to-day tactical needs and the journalism by which he tried to support his household, until his death in 1883.

His pamphlets, articles and letters during the next thirty years form a coherent commentary on contemporary political affairs in the light of his new method of analysis. They are sharp, lucid, realistic, astonishingly modern in tone, and aimed deliberately against the prevailing optimistic temper of his time.

As a revolutionary he disapproved of conspiratorial methods, which he thought obsolete and ineffective, calculated to irritate public opinion without altering its foundations, and instead set himself to create an open political party dominated by the new view of society. His later years are occupied almost exclusively with the task of gathering evidence for, and disseminating, the truths which he had discovered, until they filled the entire horizon of his followers, and became consciously woven into the texture of their every thought and word and act. For a quarter of a century he concentrated his entire being upon the attainment of this purpose, and, towards the end of his life, achieved it.

The nineteenth century contains many remarkable social critics and revolutionaries no less original, no less violent, no less dogmatic than Marx, but not one so rigorously single-minded, so absorbed in making every word and every act of his life a means towards a single, immediate, practical end, to which nothing was too sacred to sacrifice. If there is a sense in which he was born before his time, there is an equally definite sense in which he embodies one of the oldest of European traditions. For while his realism, his empiricism, his attacks on abstract principles, his demand that every solution must be tested by its applicability to, and emergence out of, the actual situation, his contempt for compromise or gradualism as modes of escape from the necessity of drastic action, his belief that the masses are infinitely gullible and must at all costs be rescued, if necessary by force, from the knaves and fools who impose upon them, make him the precursor of the severer generation of practical revolutionaries of the next century, his rigid belief in the necessity of a complete break with the past, in the need for a wholly new social system, as alone capable of saving the individual, who, if left to himself, will lose his way and perish, places him among the great authoritarian founders of new faiths, ruthless subverters and innovators who interpret the world in terms of a single, clear, passionately held principle, denouncing and destroying all that conflicts with it. His faith in his own synoptic vision of an orderly, disciplined world, destined to arise out of the inevitable self-destruction of the chaotic society of the present, was of that boundless, absolute kind which puts an end to all questions and dissolves all difficulties; which brings with it a sense of liberation similar to that which in the sixteenth and seventeenth centuries men found in the new Protestant faith, and later in the truths of science, in the principles of the great Revolution, in the systems of the German metaphysicians. If these earlier rationalists are justly called fanatical, then in this sense Marx too was a fanatic. But his faith in reason was not blind: if he appealed to reason, he appealed no less to empirical evidence. The laws of history were indeed eternal and immutable—and to grasp this fact a metaphysical intuition was required—but what they were could be established only by the evidence of empirical facts. His intellectual system was a closed one, everything that entered was made to conform to a pre-established pattern, but it was grounded on observation and experience. He was obsessed by no fixed ideas. He betrays not a trace of the notorious symptoms which accompany pathological fanaticism, that alternation of moods of sudden exaltation with a sense of loneliness and persecution, which life in wholly private worlds often engenders in those who are detached from reality.

The main ideas of his principal work appear to have matured in his mind as early as 1847. Preliminary sketches had appeared in 1849 and again ten years later, but he was incapable of beginning to write before satisfying himself that he had mastered the entire literature of his subject. This fact, together with the difficulty of finding a publisher and the necessity of providing for his own and his family's livelihood, with its accompaniment of overwork and frequent illness, put off its publication year by year. The first volume finally appeared twenty years after its conception, in 1867, and is the crowning achievement of his life. It is an attempt to give a single integrated account of the process and laws of social development, containing a complete economic theory treated historically and, less explicitly, a theory of history as determined by economic factors. It is interrupted by remarkable digressions consisting of analyses and historical sketches of the condition of the proletariat, in particular during the period of transition from manufacture to large-scale industrial capitalism, introduced to illustrate the general thesis, but in fact demonstrating a new and revolutionary method of historical writing: and in all constitutes the most formidable, sustained and elaborate indictment ever delivered against an entire social order, against its rulers, its supporters, its ideologists, its willing slaves, against all whose lives are bound up with its survival. His attack upon bourgeois society was made at a moment when it had reached the highest point of its material prosperity, in the very year in which Gladstone in a budget speech congratulated his countrymen on the 'intoxicating augmentation of their wealth and power' which recent years had witnessed, during a mood of buoyant optimism and universal confidence. In this world Marx is an isolated and bitterly hostile figure, prepared, like the early Christians, or the French revolutionaries, to reject boldly everything that it had to offer, calling its ideals worthless and its virtues vices, condemning its institutions, not because they were bad but because they were bourgeois, because they belonged to a corrupt and tyrannous society which must be annihilated totally and for ever. In an age which destroyed its adversaries by methods not less efficient because they were dignified and slow, which forced Carlyle and Schopenhauer to seek escape in a remote civilization or an idealized past, and drove its arch-enemy, Nietzsche, to hysteria and madness, Marx alone remained secure and formidable. Like an ancient prophet performing a task imposed on him by heaven, with an inner tranquillity based on clear and certain faith in the rational society of the future, he bore witness to the signs of decay and ruin which he saw on every side. The older order seemed to him to be patently crumbling before his eyes; he did more than any man to hasten the process, seeking to shorten the final agony which precedes the end.

CHAPTER II

CHILDHOOD AND ADOLESCENCE

Nimmer kann ich ruhig treiben
Was die Seele stark befasst,
Nimmer still behaglich bleiben
Und ich stürme ohne Rast.[1]

KARL MARX, *Juvenilia*

KARL HEINRICH MARX, eldest son of Heinrich and
Henrietta Marx, was born on 5 May 1818 in Trier, in
the German Rhineland, where his father practised as
a lawyer. Once the seat of a Prince-Archbishop, it
had, some fifteen years before, been occupied by the
French and was incorporated by Napoleon in the
Confederation of the Rhine. After his defeat ten years
later it was assigned by the Congress of Vienna to the
rapidly expanding Prussian kingdom.

The kings and princes of the German states whose
personal authority had recently been all but destroyed
by the successive French invasions of their territories,
were at this time busily engaged in repairing the dam-
aged fabric of hereditary monarchy, a process which
demanded the obliteration of every trace of the dangerous ideas which had begun to rouse even the placid
inhabitants of the German provinces from their
traditional lethargy. Napoleon's defeat and exile had
finally destroyed the illusions of those German radicals
who hoped that the result of Napoleon's centralizing
policy would be, if not the liberty, at any rate the unity
of Germany. The *status quo* was re-established wherever

[1] Never can I pursue in quiet that which holds my soul in
thrall, never rest at peace contented, and I storm without
cease.

this was possible; Germany was once more divided into feudally organized kingdoms and principalities, whose restored rulers, resolved to compensate themselves for the years of defeat and humiliation, set about reviving the old régime in every detail, anxious to exorcize once and for all the spectre of democratic revolution whose memory was sedulously kept alive by the more enlightened among their subjects. The King of Prussia, Frederick William III, was particularly energetic in this respect. Helped by the feudal squirearchy and such land-owning aristocracy as there was in Prussia, and following the example set by Metternich in Vienna, he succeeded in arresting the normal development of the majority of his countrymen for many years, and induced an atmosphere of profound and hopeless stagnation, beside which even France and England during the reactionary years seemed liberal and alive. This was felt most acutely by the more progressive elements in German society—not merely by the intellectuals, but by the bulk of the bourgeoisie and of the liberal aristocracy of the towns, particularly in the west, which had always preserved some contact with general European culture. It took the form of economic, social and political legislation designed to retain, and in some cases to restore, a multitude of privileges, rights and restrictions, many of them dating from the Middle Ages, sordid survivals which had long ceased to be even picturesque; and, since they were in direct conflict with the needs of the new age, they needed and obtained an elaborate and ruinous structure of tariffs to keep them in being. This led to a policy of systematic discouragement of trade and industry and, since the obsolete structure had to be preserved against popular pressure, to the creation of a despotic officialdom, whose task it was to insulate German society from the contaminating influence of liberal ideas and institutions.

The increased power of the police, the introduction of rigid supervision over all departments of public and private life, provoked a literature of protest which was rigorously suppressed by the government censors. German writers and poets went into voluntary exile, and from Paris or Switzerland conducted passionate propaganda against the régime. The general situation was reflected particularly clearly in the condition of that section of society which throughout the nineteenth century tended to act as the most sensitive barometer of the direction of social change—the small but widely scattered Jewish population.

The Jews had every reason to feel grateful to Napoleon; wherever he appeared he set himself to destroy the traditional edifice of social rank and privilege, of racial, political and religious barriers, putting in its place his newly promulgated legal code, which claimed as the source of its authority the principles of reason and human equality. This act, by opening to the Jews the doors of trades and professions which had hitherto remained rigidly barred to them, had the effect of releasing a mass of imprisoned energy and ambition, and led to the enthusiastic—in some cases over-enthusiastic—acceptance of general European culture by a hitherto segregated community, which from that day became a new and important factor in the evolution of European society.

Some of these liberties were later withdrawn by Napoleon himself, and what was left of them was for the most part revoked by the restored German princes, with the result that many Jews who had eagerly broken away from the traditional mode of life led by their fathers toward the prospects of a wider existence, now found that the avenue which had so suddenly been half-opened before them had as suddenly become barred again, and consequently were confronted with a difficult choice. They had either to retrace their steps and painfully re-enter the Ghetto in which their families for the most part still continued to live, or else, altering their names and religion, to start new lives as German patriots and members of the Christian Church. The case of Herschel Levi was typical of a whole generation. His father, Marx Levi, and his father before him, were Rabbis in the Rhineland, who, like the great majority of their fellow Jews, had passed their entire existence within the confines of a pious, inbred, passionately self-centred community, which, faced with the hostility of its Christian neighbours, had taken refuge behind a defensive wall of pride and suspicion which had for centuries almost wholly preserved them from contact with the changing life outside. The enlightenment had, nevertheless, begun to penetrate even this artificial enclave of the Middle Ages, and Herschel, who had received a secular education, became a disciple of the French rationalists and their disciples, the German *illuminati*, and was early in life converted to the religion of reason and humanity. He accepted it with candour and naïveté, nor did the long years of darkness and reaction succeed in shaking his faith in God and his simple and optimistic humanitarianism. He detached himself completely from his family, changed his name to Heinrich Marx, and acquired new friends and new interests. His legal practice was moderately successful, and he began to look to a settled future as the head of a respectable German bourgeois family, when the anti-Jewish laws of 1816 suddenly cut off his means of livelihood.

He probably felt no exceptional reverence for the established church, but he was even less attached to the Synagogue, and, holding vaguely deist views, saw no moral or social obstacle to complete conformity with the mildly enlightened Lutheranism of his Prussian neighbours. At any rate if he did hesitate, it was not for long. He was officially received into the Church early in 1817, a year before the birth of his eldest son, Karl. The hostility of the latter to everything connected with religion, and in particular with Judaism, may well be partly due to the peculiar and embarrassed situation in which such converts sometimes found themselves. Some escaped by becoming devout and even fanatical Christians, others by rebelling against all established religion. They suffered in proportion to their sensitiveness and intelligence. Both Heine and Disraeli were all their lives obsessed by the personal problem of their peculiar status; they neither renounced nor accepted it completely, but alternately mocked at and defended the religion of their fathers, incapable of a single-minded attitude towards their ambiguous position, perpetually suspicious of latent contempt or condescension concealed beneath the fiction of their complete acceptance by the society in which they lived.

The elder Marx suffered from none of these complications. He was a simple, serious, well-educated man, but he was neither conspicuously intelligent nor abnormally sensitive. A disciple of Leibnitz and Voltaire, Lessing and Kant, he possessed in addition a gentle,

timid and accommodating temper, and ultimately
became a passionate Prussian patriot and monarchist, a
position which he sought to justify by pointing to the
figure of Frederick the Great—in his view a tolerant
and enlightened prince who compared favourably with
Napoleon, with his notorious contempt for ideologists.
After his baptism he adopted the Christian name of
Heinrich, and educated his family as liberal protestants,
faithful to the existing order and to the reigning King of
Prussia. Anxious as he was to identify that ruler with
the ideal prince depicted by his favourite philosophers,
the repulsive figure of Frederick William III defeated
even his loyal imagination. Indeed, the only occasion
on which this tremulous and retiring man is known to
have behaved with courage, was a public dinner at
which he made a speech on the desirability of moderate
social and political reforms worthy of a wise and benevolent ruler. This swiftly drew upon him the attention of
the Prussian police. Heinrich Marx at once retracted
everything, and convinced everyone of his complete
harmlessness. It is not improbable that this slight but
humiliating *contretemps*, and in particular his father's
craven and submissive attitude, made a definite impression on Karl, then sixteen years old, and left behind it
a smouldering sense of resentment which later events
fanned into a flame.

His father had early become aware that while his
other children were in no way remarkable, in Karl he
had an unusual and difficult son; with a sharp and
lucid intelligence he combined a stubborn and domi-
neering temper, a truculent love of independence,
exceptional emotional restraint, and over all a colossal,
ungovernable intellectual appetite. The timorous

lawyer, whose life was spent in social and personal compromise, was puzzled and frightened by his son's intransigeance which, in his opinion, was bound to antagonize important persons, and might, one day, lead him into serious trouble. He frequently and anxiously begged him in his letters to moderate his enthusiasms, to impose some sort of discipline on himself, to cultivate polite, civilized habits, not to neglect possible benefactors, above all not to estrange everyone by violently refusing to adapt himself—in short to satisfy the elementary requirements of the society in which he was to live his life. But these letters, even at their most disapproving, remained gentle and affectionate; in spite of growing uneasiness about his character and career, Heinrich Marx treated his son with an instinctive delicacy, and never attempted to oppose or bully him on any serious issue. Consequently their relations continued to be warm, intimate and grave until the death of the older Marx in 1838.

It seems certain that the father had a definite influence on his son's intellectual development. The elder Marx believed with Condorcet that man is by nature both good and rational, and that all that is needed to ensure the triumph of these qualities is the removal of unnatural obstacles from his path. They were disappearing already, and disappearing fast, and the time was rapidly approaching when the last citadels of reaction, the Catholic Church and the feudal nobility, would melt away before the irresistible march of reason. Social, political, religious, racial barriers were so many artificial products of the deliberate obscurantism of priests and rulers; with their disappearance a new day would dawn for the human race, when all men would be equal, not only politically and legally, in their formal, external relations, but socially and personally, in their most intimate daily intercourse.

His own history seemed to him to corroborate this triumphantly. Born a Jew, a citizen of inferior legal and social status, he had attained to equality with his more enlightened neighbours, had earned their respect as a human being, and had become assimilated into what appeared to him as their more rational and dignified mode of life. He believed that a new day was dawning in the history of human emancipation, in the light of which his children would live their lives as free-born citizens in a just and liberal state. Elements of this belief are clearly apparent in his son's social doctrine. Karl Marx did not, indeed, believe in the power of rational argument to influence action, but there is, nevertheless, a definite sense in which he remained both a rationalist and a perfectibilian to the end of his life. He believed in the complete intelligibility of the process of social evolution; he believed that society is inevitably progressive, that its movement from stage to stage is a forward movement, that each successive stage represents development, is nearer the rational ideal than its precursors. He detested, as passionately as any eighteenth-century thinker, emotionalism, belief in supernatural causes, visionary fantasy of every kind, and systematically under-estimated the influence of such non-rational forces as nationalism, and religious and racial solidarity. Although, therefore, it remains true that the Hegelian philosophy is the greatest single formative influence in his life, the principles of philosophical rationalism which were planted in him by his father and his father's friends, performed a definite work of inoculation, so that when later he encountered the romantic metaphysical systems developed by Fichte and Hegel, he was saved from that total surrender to their fascination which undid so many of his contemporaries. It was this pronounced taste, acquired early in life, for lucid argument and an empirical approach, that enabled him to preserve a measure of independence in the face of the prevalent philosophy, and later to alter it to his own more positivist pattern. This may perhaps account for his pronounced anti-romantic tendency, so sharply different from the outlook common to such leading radicals of his time as Börne, Heine, or Lassalle, whose origins and education are in many respects closely analogous to his own.

Little is known of his childhood and early years in Trier. His mother played a singularly small part in his life; she belonged to a family of Hungarian Jews settled in Holland, where her father was a Rabbi, and was a solid and uneducated woman entirely absorbed in the cares of her large household, who did not at any time show the slightest understanding of her son's gifts or inclinations, was shocked by his radicalism, and in later years appears to have lost all interest in his existence. Of the eight children of Heinrich and Henrietta Marx Karl was the second; apart from a mild affection as a child for his eldest sister Sophia, he showed little interest in his brothers and sisters either then or later. He was sent to the local High School where he obtained equal praise for his industry and the high-minded and earnest tone of his essays on moral and religious topics. He was moderately proficient in mathematics and theology, but his main interests were literary and artistic: a tendency due principally to the influence of two men from whom he learned most and of whom all his life he spoke with affection and respect. The first of these was his father; the other was Freiherr Ludwig von Westphalen who lived in the same street as Heinrich Marx and was on friendly terms with the amiable lawyer and his family. Westphalen belonged to that educated and liberal section of the German upper class whose representatives were to be found in the vanguard of every enlightened and progressive movement in their country in the first half of the nineteenth century. He was a distinguished Prussian government official, and an attractive and cultivated man. He belonged to the generation dominated by the great figures of Goethe, Schiller and Hölderlin, and under their influence had wandered beyond the aesthetic frontiers so strictly established by the literary mandarins in Paris, and shared in the growing German passion for the rediscovered genius of Dante, Shakespeare, Homer and the Greek tragedians. He was attracted by the striking ability and eager receptiveness of Heinrich Marx's son, encouraged him to read, lent him books, took him for walks in the neighbouring woods and talked to him about Æschylus, Cervantes, Shakespeare, quoting long passages to his enthusiastic listener. Karl, who reached maturity at a very early age, became a devoted reader of the new romantic literature: the taste he acquired during these impressionable years remained unaltered until his death. He was in later life fond of recalling his evenings with Westphalen, during what seemed to him to have been the happiest period of his life. He had been treated by a man much older than himself on terms of equality at a time when he was in particular need of sympathy and encouragement; when one tactless or insulting act might have left a lasting mark, he was received with rare courtesy and hospitality. His doctorate thesis contains a glowing dedication to Westphalen, full of gratitude and admiration. In 1837 Marx asked for the hand of his daughter in marriage and obtained his consent without difficulty; an act which, owing to the great difference in their social condition, is said to have dismayed her relations. Speaking of Westphalen in later life Marx, whose judgements of men are not noted for their generosity, grew almost sentimental. Westphalen had humanized and strengthened that belief in himself and his own powers which was at all periods Marx's single most outstanding characteristic. He is one of the rare revolutionaries who were neither thwarted nor persecuted in their early life. Consequently, in spite of his abnormal sensitiveness, his *amour-propre*, his vanity, his aggressiveness and his arrogance, it is a singularly unbroken, positive and self-confident figure that faces us during forty years of illness, poverty and unceasing warfare.

He left the Trier school at the age of seventeen, and, following his father's advice, in the autumn of 1835 became a student in the faculty of law in the University of Bonn. Here he seems to have been entirely happy: he announced that he proposed to attend at least seven courses of weekly lectures, among them lectures on Homer by the celebrated Schlegel, lectures on mythology, on Latin poetry, on modern art. He lived the gay and dissipated life of the ordinary German student, played an active part in university societies, wrote Byronic poems, got into debt and on at least one occasion was arrested by the authorities for riotous behaviour. At the end of the summer term of 1836 he left Bonn and in the autumn was transferred to the University of Berlin.

This event marks a sharp crisis in his life. The conditions under which he had lived hitherto had been comparatively provincial: Trier was a small and pretty town which had survived from an older order, untouched by the great social and economic revolution which was changing the contour of the civilized world: the growing industrial development of Cologne and Düsseldorf seemed infinitely remote; no urgent problems, social, intellectual, or material, had troubled the peace of the gentle and cultivated milieu of his father's friends, a placid preserve of the eighteenth century which had artificially survived into the nineteenth. By comparison with Trier or Bonn, Berlin was an immensely large and populous city, modern, ugly, pretentious and intensely serious, at once the centre of the Prussian bureaucracy and the meeting-place of the discontented radical intellectuals who formed the nucleus of the growing opposition to it. Marx retained all his life a considerable capacity for enjoyment and a strong if rather ponderous sense of fun, but no one could even at that time describe him as superficial or frivolous. He was sobered by the tense and tragic atmosphere in which he suddenly felt himself, and with his accustomed energy began at once to explore and criticize his new environment.

CHAPTER III

THE PHILOSOPHY OF THE SPIRIT

Was Ihr den Geist der Zeiten heisst
Das ist im Grund der Herren eigner **Geist**
In dem die Zeiten sich bespiegeln.

(What you call the spirit of the age is in reality one's own
spirit, in which the age is mirrored.)

GOETHE

La raison a toujours raison.
(Reason is always right.)

I

THE dominant intellectual influence in the University
of Berlin, as indeed in every other German university
at this time, was the Hegelian philosophy. The soil
for this had been prepared by gradual revolt from the
beliefs and idiom of the classical period, which had
begun in the seventeenth, and was consolidated and
reduced to a system in the eighteenth century. The
greatest and most original figure in this movement
among the Germans was Gottfried Wilhelm Leibnitz,
whose ideas were developed by his followers and interpreters into a coherent and dogmatic metaphysical
system, which, so their popularizers claimed, was
logically demonstrable by deductive steps from simple
premises, in their turn self-evident to those who could
use that infallible intellectual intuition with which all
thinking beings were endowed at birth. This rigid
intellectualism was attacked in England, where no form
of pure rationalism had ever found a congenial soil,
by the most influential philosophical writers of the age.

Locke, Hume, and, towards the end of the century,
Bentham and the philosophical radicals agreed in denying the existence of any such faculty as an intellectual
intuition into the real nature of things. No faculty other
than the familiar physical senses could provide that
initial empirical information on which all other knowledge of the world is ultimately founded. Since all
information was conveyed by the senses, reason could
not be an independent source of knowledge, and was
responsible only for arranging, classifying and fitting
together such information, and drawing deductions from
it, operating upon material obtained without its aid. In
France the rationalist position was attacked by the
materialist school in the eighteenth century, and while
Voltaire and Diderot, Condillac and Helvétius freely
acknowledged their debt to the free-thinking English,
they constructed an independent system whose influence
on European thought and action continues into the
present day. Some did not go to the length of denying
the existence of knowledge obtained otherwise than by
senses, but claimed that, though such innate knowledge
itself exists and indeed reveals valuable truth, it provides
no evidence for the propositions whose incontrovertible
truth the older rationalists claimed to know, a fact which
careful and scrupulous mental self-examination would
show to any open-minded man not blinded by religious
dogmatism or political and ethical prejudice. Too many
abuses had been defended by appeals to authority,
or to a special intuition: thus Aristotle, appealing to
reason for confirmation, had maintained that men were
by nature unequal, that some were naturally slaves,
others free men; and so too the Bible, which taught
that truth could be revealed by supernatural means,

afforded texts which could be invoked to prove that man was naturally vicious and must be curbed—theses used by reactionary governments to support the existing state of political, social, even moral inequality. But experience and reason, properly understood, combined to show the precise opposite of this. Arguments could be produced to show beyond any possible doubt that man was naturally good, that reason existed equally in all sentient beings, that the cause of all oppression and suffering was human ignorance, produced partly by social and material conditions, which arose in the course of natural historical development, partly through the deliberate suppression of the truth by ambitious tyrants and unscrupulous priests, most frequently by the interplay of both. These influences could, however, by the action of an enlightened and benevolent government, be exposed and thereby annihilated. For, left to themselves, with no obstacles to obscure their vision and to frustrate their endeavours, men would pursue virtue and knowledge; justice and equality would take the place of authority and privilege, competition would yield to co-operation, happiness and wisdom would become universal possessions. The central tenet of this semi-empirical rationalism consisted in boundless faith in the power of reason to explain and improve the world, all previous failure to do so being explained as a result of ignorance of the laws which regulate the behaviour of nature, animate and inanimate. Misery is the result of ignorance not only of nature but of the laws of social behaviour. To abolish it one measure is both necessary and sufficient: the employment of reason and of reason alone in the conduct of human affairs.

This task is admittedly far from easy; men have lived

too long in a world of intellectual darkness to be able to move unblinkered in the sudden light of day. A process of gradual education in scientific principles is therefore required: the growth of reason and the advance of truth, while in themselves sufficient to conquer the forces of prejudice and ignorance, cannot occur until enlightened men are found ready to devote their whole lives to the task of educating the vast benighted mass of mankind.

But here a new obstacle arises: whereas the original cause of human misery, neglect of reason and intellectual indolence, was not deliberately brought about, there exists in our own day and has existed for many centuries past, a class of men who, perceiving that their own power rests on ignorance which blinds men to its injustice, promote it by every invention and means in their power. By nature all men are rational, and all rational beings have equal rights before the natural law of reason. But the ruling classes, the princes, the nobility, the priests, the generals, realize only too well that the spread of reason would soon open the eyes of the peoples of the world to the colossal fraud by which in the name of such hollow figments as the sanctity of the church, the divine right of kings, the claims of national pride or possession, they are forced to give up their natural claims, and labour uncomplainingly for the maintenance of a small class which has no shadow of right to exact such privilege. It is therefore in the direct personal interest of the upper class in the social hierarchy to thwart the growth of natural knowledge, wherever it threatens to expose the arbitrary character of its authority, and in its place to substitute a dogmatic code, a row of unintelligible mysteries expressed in high-sounding phrases with which to confuse the feeble intelligences of their unhappy subjects, and keep them in a state of blind obedience. Even though some among the ruling class may be genuinely self-deceived and come themselves to believe in their own inventions, some there must be who know that only by systematic deception, propped up by the occasional use of violence, could so corrupt and unnatural an order be preserved. It is the first duty, therefore, of an enlightened ruler to break the power of the privileged classes, and to allow natural reason with which all men are endowed to re-assert itself; and since reason can never be opposed to reason, all private and public conflict is ultimately due to some irrational element, some simple failure to perceive how an harmonious adjustment of apparently opposed interests may be made.

Reason is always right. To every question there is only one true answer which with sufficient assiduity can be infallibly discovered, and this applies no less to questions of ethics or politics, of personal and social life, than to the problems of physics or mathematics. Once found, the putting of a solution into practice is a matter of mere technical skill; but the traditional enemies of progress must first be removed, and men taught the importance of acting in all questions on the advice of disinterested scientific experts, whose knowledge is founded on reason and experience. Once this has been achieved, the path is clear to the millennium.

But the influence of environment is no less important than that of education. If you would wish to foretell the course of a man's life, you must consider such factors as the character of the region in which he lives, its climate, the fertility of its soil, its distance from the sea, in addition to his physical characteristics and the nature of his daily occupation. Man is an object in nature, and the human soul, like material substance, is swayed by no supernatural influences and possesses no occult properties; its entire behaviour can be adequately accounted for by means of ordinary verifiable physical hypotheses. The French materialist, La Mettrie, developed this empiricism to its fullest limits in a celebrated treatise, *L'Homme Machine*, which caused an immense scandal at the time of its publication. His views were shared in various degrees by the editors of the Encyclopaedia, Diderot and d'Alembert, by Holbach, Helvétius and Condillac, who, whatever their other differences, were agreed that man's principal difference from the plants and lower animals lies in his possession of self-consciousness, that is awareness of certain of his own processes, in his capacity to use reason and imagination, to conceive ideal purposes and to attach moral values to this or that activity or characteristic in accordance with its tendency to forward or retard the ends which he desired to realize. A serious paradox which this view involved was the conflict between free-will on the one hand, and complete determination by character and environment on the other; which was the old conflict between free-will and divine foreknowledge in a new form, with Nature in the place of God. Spinoza had observed that if a stone falling through the air could think, it might well imagine that it had freely chosen its own path, being unaware of the external causes such as the aim and force of the thrower and the natural medium which determine its fall. Similarly, it is only his ignorance of the natural causes of his behaviour which makes man suppose himself in some fashion different from the falling stone: omniscience would quickly dispel this vain delusion, even though the feeling of freedom to which it gives rise may itself persist, having lost its power to deceive. So far as extreme empiricism is concerned, this deterministic doctrine is entirely consistent with optimistic rationalism: but it carries the very opposite implications with regard to the possibility of reform in human affairs. For if men are made saints or criminals solely by the movement of matter in space, the educators are as rigorously determined to act as they do, as those whom it is their duty to educate. Everything occurs as it does as a result of unalterable processes of nature; and no improvement can be effected by the free decisions of individuals, however wise, however benevolent and powerful, since they, no more than any other entity, can alter natural necessity. This celebrated crux, stripped of its old theological dress, emerged even more sharply in its secular form; it presented equal difficulties to both sides, but became obscured by the larger issues at stake. Atheists, sceptics, materialists, rationalists, utilitarians, belonged to one camp; theists, metaphysicians, supporters and apologists of the existing order to the other; the rift between enlightenment and clericalism was so great, and the war between them so savage, that doctrinal difficulties within each camp passed relatively unperceived.

It is the first of the two theses that became the fundamental doctrine of the radical intellectuals of the next century. They emphasized the natural goodness of men unspoiled by a bad or ignorant government, and emphasized the immense power of rational education to rescue the masses of mankind from their present miseries, to institute a juster and more scientific distribution

of the world's goods, and so to lead humanity
to the limits of attainable happiness. The imagination
of the eighteenth century was dominated by the
phenomenal strides made by the mathematical and
physical sciences during the previous century, and it
was a natural step to apply the method which had proved
so successful in the hands of Kepler and Galileo,
Descartes and Newton, to the interpretation of social
phenomena and to the conduct of life. If any single
individual may be said to have created this movement, it is unquestionably Voltaire. If he was not its
originator, he was its greatest and most celebrated
protagonist for more than half a century. His books,
his pamphlets, his mere existence did incomparably
more to destroy the hold of absolutism and catholicism
than any other single factor. Nor did his death arrest
his influence. Freedom of thought was identified with
his name: its battles were fought under his banner:
no popular revolution from his day to ours has failed
to draw some of its most effective weapons from that
inexhaustible armoury which two centuries have not
rendered obsolete. But if Voltaire created the religion
of man, Rousseau was the greatest of its prophets. He
was a preacher and a propagandist of genius, and gave
it a new eloquence and ardour, a richer, vaguer and
more emotionally charged language, which profoundly
affected the writers and thinkers of the nineteenth
century. Indeed, he may be said to have created the
new modes of thought and of feeling, a wholly new
idiom, which was adopted as their natural vehicle of
self-expression by the artistic and social rebels of the
nineteenth century, the first generation of romantics
who sought inspiration in the revolutionary history and

literature of France and in her name raised the banner of revolt in their own backward lands.

One of the most fervent and certainly the most effective among the advocates of this doctrine in England was the idealistic Welsh manufacturer, Robert Owen. His creed was summarized in the sentence inscribed at the head of his journal, *The New Moral World*: 'Any general character, from the best to the worst, from the most ignorant to the most enlightened, may be given to any community, even the world at large, by the application of proper means, which means are to a great extent at the command and under the control of those who have influence in the affairs of men.' He had triumphantly demonstrated the truth of his theory by extablishing model conditions in his own cotton mills in New Lanark, limiting working hours, and creating provision for health and a savings fund. By this means he increased the productivity of his factory and raised immensely the standard of living of his workers, and what was even more impressive to the outside world, trebled his own fortune. New Lanark became a centre of pilgrimage for kings and statesmen, and, as the first successful experiment in peaceful co-operation between labour and capital, had a considerable influence on the history both of socialism and of the working class. His later attempts at practical reform were less successful. Owen, who died in deep old age in the middle of the nineteenth century, was the last survivor of the classical period of rationalism, and, his faith unshaken by repeated failures, until the end of his life believed in the omnipotence of education and the perfectibility of man.

The effect which the victorious advance of the new

ideas had upon European culture is hardly inferior to that of the Italian Renaissance. The spirit of free inquiry into personal and social issues, of calling all things in question before the bar of reason, acquired a formal discipline and an increasingly enthusiastic acceptance in wide sections of society. Intellectual courage, and even more, intellectual disinterestedness, became fashionable virtues. Voltaire and Rousseau were universally fêted and admired, Hume was magnificently received in Paris. This was the climate of opinion which formed the character of the revolutionaries of 1789, a severe and heroic generation which yields to none in the clearness and purity of its convictions, in the robust and unsentimental intelligence of its humanism—above all, in its absolute moral and intellectual integrity securely founded upon the belief that the truth must ultimately prevail because it is the truth, a belief which years of exile and persecution did not weaken. Their moral and political ideas, and their words of praise and blame have long since become the common inheritance of democrats of all shades and hues; socialists and liberals, utilitarians and believers in natural rights, speak their language and profess their faith, not so naïvely, nor with such utter confidence, but also less eloquently, less simply and less convincingly.

The counter-attack came with the turn of the century. It grew on German soil, but soon spread over the whole civilized world, checking the advance of empiricism from the west, and putting in its place a profoundly metaphysical view of nature and of the individual, the effects of which are with us still, and growing in strength and influence. Germany, spiritually and materially crippled by the Thirty Years' War, was, at the end of a long and sterile period, beginning to produce once more, towards the end of the eighteenth century, an indigenous culture of its own, influenced by, but fundamentally independent of, the French models which all Europe vied in imitating. Both in philosophy and in criticism the Germans began to produce works which were in form clumsier, but more ardently felt, more vehemently expressed, and more disquieting than anything written in France outside the pages of Rousseau; the French saw in this rich disarray only a grotesque travesty of their own limpid style and exquisite symmetry. The Napoleonic Wars which added to the Germans' wounded intellectual pride the humiliation of military defeat, made the rift still wider, and the strong patriotic reaction which began during these wars and rose to a wild flood of national feeling after Napoleon's defeat, became identified with the new, so-called romantic philosophy of Kant's successors, Fichte, Schelling and Hegel, which thus obtained national significance and became broadened and popularized into an almost official German faith. Against the scientific empiricism of the French and English, the Germans put forward the metaphysical historicism of Herder and of Hegel. Founded on the criticism of its rivals, it offered a bold alternative, the influence of which altered the history of civilization in Europe and left an ineffaceable impression on its imagination and modes of feeling.

The classical philosophers of the eighteenth century had asked: Given that man is neither more nor less than an object in nature, what are the laws which govern his behaviour? If it is possible to discover by empirical means under what conditions bodies fall, planets rotate, trees grow, ice turns into water and water into steam, it must be no less possible to find out under what conditions men are caused to eat, drink, sleep, love, hate, fight one another, constitute themselves into families, tribes, nations, and again into monarchies, oligarchies, democracies. Until this is discovered by a Newton or a Galileo, no true science of society can come into being. This radical empiricism appeared to Hegel to embody a scientific dogmatism even more disastrous than the theology which it wished to displace, involving the fallacy that only methods successful in the natural sciences can be valid in every other department of experience. He was sceptical of the new method even in the case of the material world, and quite groundlessly suspected natural scientists of arbitrarily selecting the phenomena which they discussed and no less arbitrarily limiting themselves to certain kinds of evidence alone. But if his attitude towards empiricism in the sciences was unsympathetic, he spoke with even greater violence of its ruinous consequences when applied to the subject of human history. If history were written in accordance with scientific rules, as the word was understood by Voltaire or by Hume, a monstrous distortion of the facts would result, which the best historians of the past, Hume and Voltaire themselves, indeed, when they were not theorizing but writing history, had unconsciously avoided by a sure historical intuition. He conceived of history as it were in two dimensions: the horizontal, in which the phenomena of different spheres of activity, occurring among different peoples belonging to the same stage of development, are seen to be broadly interconnected in some unitary pattern, which gives each period its own individual, immediately recognizable character; and the vertical dimension, in which the same cross-section of events is viewed as part of a temporal succession, as a necessary stage in a developing process, in some sense contained by its predecessor in time, which is itself seen already to embody, although in a less developed state, those very tendencies and forces whose full emergence makes the later age that which it ultimately comes to be. Hence every age, if it is to be genuinely understood, must be considered in relation not to the past alone; for it contains within its womb seeds of the future, foreshadowing the contour of what is yet to come; and this relation, no historian, however scrupulous, however anxious to avoid straying beyond the bare evidence of the facts, can allow himself to ignore. Only so can he represent in correct perspective the elements which compose the period with which he is dealing, distinguishing the significant from the trivial, the central, determining characteristics of an age from those accidental, adventitious elements in it, which might have happened anywhere and at any time, and consequently have no deep roots in its particular past, and no appreciable effects on its particular future.

The conception of growth by which the acorn is said potentially to contain the oak, and can be adequately described only in terms of such development, is a doctrine as old as Aristotle and indeed older. In the Renaissance it came to light once more and was developed to its fullest extent by Leibnitz, who taught that the universe was compounded of a plurality of independent individual substances, each of which is to be conceived as composed of its own whole past and its own whole future. Nothing was accidental; no object could be described as the empiricists wished to describe it, namely as a succession of continuous or discontinuous phenomena or states, connected at best only by the external relation of mechanical causation. The only true definition of an object was in terms which explained why it necessarily developed as it did in terms of its individual history, as a growing entity, each stage of which was, in the words of Leibnitz, '*chargé du passé et gros de l'avenir*'. Leibnitz made no detailed attempt to apply this metaphysical doctrine to historical events, and yet that seemed to Hegel to be the sphere to which it best applied. For unless some relation other than that of scientific causation be postulated, it seems impossible to account for, even to express, the entirely individual character of a particular personality or period of history, the individual essence of a particular work of art or of science, each of whose characteristics may indeed closely resemble something which has occurred before or after it, but whose totality is in some sense unique, and exists only once; and cannot therefore be accounted for by a scientific method whose successful application depends upon the occurrence of the precise opposite, namely, that the same phenomenon, the same combination of characteristics should repeat itself, regularly recur, again and again.

The new method was first triumphantly applied by Herder, who, under the influence perhaps of the growth of national and racial self-consciousness in Europe, and moved by hatred of the levelling cosmopolitanism and universalism of the prevailing French philosophy, applied the concept of organic development (as it later came to be called) to the history of entire cultures and nations as well as individuals. Indeed, he represented it as more fundamental in the case of the former, since individuals can only properly be viewed as occurring at a particular stage of the development of a society, which, in the thought and action of its greatest sons, reaches its most typical expression. He immersed himself therefore in the study of national German culture, its barbarian beginnings, its philology and archaeology, its medieval history and institutions, its traditional folklore and antiquities. From this he attempted to draw a portrait of the living German spirit, as a formative force responsible for the unity of its own peculiar national development, which cannot be accounted for by the crudely empirical relation of mere loose before-and-afterness in time, by which the uniform, monotonous history of mechanically caused events, the rotation of the crops or the yearly revolutions of the earth, may perhaps be satisfactorily explained.

Hegel developed this still more widely and ambitiously. He taught that the explanation offered by French materialism afforded at best a hypothesis for explaining some static but no dynamic phenomena, differences but not change. Given such and such material conditions, it may be possible to predict that the men born in them will develop certain characteristics, directly attributable to physical causes and to the education given to them by previous generations, themselves affected by the same conditions. But even if this is so, how much does it really tell us? The physical conditions of Italy, for example, were much the same in the first as they were in the eighth and fifteenth centuries, and yet the ancient Romans differ widely from their Italian descendants, and the men of the Renaissance showed certain marked characteristics, which Italy in decline was losing or had totally lost. It cannot therefore be these relatively invariant conditions, with which alone the natural scientists are competent to deal, that are responsible for the phenomena of historical change, for progress and reaction, glory and decline. Some dynamic factor must be postulated to account both for change as such and for the single, clearly perceptible, direction which it has. Such change is plainly not repetitive: each age inherits something new from its predecessors, in virtue of which it differs from every preceding period; the principle of development excludes the principle of uniform repetition which is the foundation on which Galileo and Newton built. If history possesses laws, these laws must evidently be different in kind from what has passed for the only possible pattern of scientific law so far: and since everything that is, persists, and has some history, the laws of history must for that very reason be identical with the laws of being of everything that exists.

Where is this principle of historical motion to be found? It is a confession of human failure, of the defeat of reason, to declare that this dynamic principle is that notorious object of the empiricist's gibes, a mysterious and occult power which men cannot expect even to detect. It would be strange if that which governs our normal lives were not more present to us, a more familiar experience than any other that we have. For we need only take our own lives as the microcosm and pattern of the universe. We speak familiarly enough of the character, or of the temper, of a man as accounting for his acts and thoughts, not as some independent thing totally distinct from them, but as the common pattern which they express: and the better we say we know a man, the better we may be said to know his moral and mental constitution in its relation to the external world. Hegel transferred the concept of the personal character of the individual which gradually unfolds itself throughout a man's life, to the case of entire cultures and nations: he referred to it variously as the Idea or Spirit, distinguished stages in its evolution, and pronounced it to be the motive, dynamic factor in the development of specific peoples and civilizations and so of the sentient universe as a whole. Further, he taught that the error of all previous thinkers was to assume the relative independence of different spheres of activity at a given period, of the wars of an age from its art, of its philosophy from its daily life. We should not naturally make this separation in the case of individuals; in the case of those with whom we are best acquainted, we half-unconsciously correlate all their acts as different manifestations of a single nature; we are affected by innumerable data drawn from this or that phase of their activity, which collectively influence our mental portrait of them. This, according to Hegel, applies no less to our concept of a culture or a particular historical period. The historians of the past have tended to write monographs on the history of this or that city or campaign, of the acts of this or that king or commander, as if they could be represented in isolation from the other phenomena of their time. But just as the acts of an individual are the acts of the whole individual, so the cultural phenomena of an age, the particular pattern of events which constitute it, are expressions of the whole age and of its whole personality, a fact which we do indeed tacitly recognize in speaking of a phenomenon as typical of the ancient rather than the modern world, or of an age of chaos rather than of one of settled peace.

This should be recognized explicitly. In writing, for instance, the history of seventeenth-century music, and in considering the rise of a particular form of polyphony, it is relevant to ask whether a development of a similar pattern may not be observed in the history of science at this time; whether, for example, the discovery of the differential calculus simultaneously by Newton and Leibnitz was purely accidental, or due to certain general characteristics of that particular stage of European culture, which produced a not dissimilar genius in Bach and Leibnitz, in Milton and Poussin. Obsession with rigorous scientific method might lead historians, as it does natural scientists, to build walls between their fields of inquiry and treat each branch of human activity as functioning in relative isolation, like so many parallel streams which cross rarely and without effect; whereas, if the historian is fully to realize his task, to rise above the chronicler and the antiquary, he must endeavour to paint a portrait of an age in movement, to collect that which is characteristic, distinguish between its component elements, between the old and the new, the fruitful and the sterile, the dying survivals of a previous age and the heralds of the future, born before their time.

This command to look in the particular for the most vivid expression of the universal, for the concrete, the differentiated, the individual, to emulate the art and the realism of the biographer and the painter rather than the photographer and the statistician, is the peculiar legacy of Hegel. If history is a science, it must not be beguiled by the false analogy of physics or mathematics, which, looking for the widest obtainable, least varying, common characteristics, deliberately ignores what specifically belongs to only one time and one place, seeking to be as general, as abstract, as formal, as possible. The historian, on the contrary, must see and describe phenomena in their fullest context, against the background of the past and the foreground of the future, as being organic to all other phenomena which springs from the same cultural impulse.

The effect of this doctrine, at once a symptom and a cause of a change of outlook on the part of an entire generation, and now grown so familiar, is inestimably great. Our habit of attaching particular characteristics to particular periods and places and of seeing individuals or their acts as typical of nations or of times: of bestowing almost a personality of their own, active causal properties, upon certain periods or peoples, or even on widely felt social attitudes, in virtue of which acts are described as expressions of the spirit of the Renaissance or of the French Revolution, of German romanticism or of the Victorian Age, springs from this new historicism of outlook. Hegel's specifically logical doctrines and his view of the method of the natural sciences were barren and their effects were wholly disastrous. His true importance lies in his influence in the field of social and historical studies, in the creation of a new science which consists in the history and criticism of human institutions, viewed as great collective quasi-personalities, which possess a life and character of their own, and cannot be described purely in terms of the individuals who compose them. It was largely due to his influence that there came into existence a new school of German historians whose work made all writers who explained events as the outcome of the character or intentions, the personal defeat or triumph of this or that king or statesman, seem naïve and unscientific.

If history is the development of the impersonal Spirit, which Hegel did not identify solely with the human spirit, since he denied any essential divorce between mind and matter, it is necessary to rewrite it as the history of the achievement of the Spirit. The horizon suddenly seemed immensely widened. Legal history ceased to be a remote and special preserve of archaeologists and antiquaries and was transformed into Historical Jurisprudence, wherein contemporary legal institutions were interpreted as an orderly evolution from Roman or earlier law, embodying the Spirit of the Law in itself, of society in its legal aspect, interwoven with political, religious, social aspects of its life.

Henceforth the history of art and the history of philosophy began to be treated as complementary and indispensable elements in the general history of culture: facts previously thought trivial or sordid were accorded sudden importance as being hitherto unexplored domains of the activity of the Spirit—the history of trade, of dress, of the useful arts were seen to be essential elements in the complete, 'organic', institutional history of mankind.

There was one respect, however, in which Hegel sharply diverged from the Leibnitzian conception of development as a smooth progression of an essence gradually unfolding itself from potentiality into actuality. He insisted on the reality and necessity of conflicts and wars and revolutions, of the tragic waste and destruction in the world. He declared that every process is one of perpetual tension between two incompatible forces each straining against the other, and by this mutual conflict advancing their own development; this duel—which is sometimes concealed and sometimes open, and can be traced in all provinces of conscious activity as the struggle between so many rival physical, moral and intellectual forces and influences—grows in strength and sharpness until it turns into an open conflict, which culminates in a final collision, the violence of which destroys both the adversaries. This is the point at which the hitherto continuous development is broken, a sudden leap takes place to a new level, where-upon the tension between a new dyad of forces begins once more. Certain among those leaps, those, namely, which occur on a sufficiently large and noticeable scale, are termed political revolutions. But, on a more trivial scale, they occur in every sphere of activity, in the arts and sciences, in the growth of physical organisms studied by biologists and in the atomic processes studied by chemists, and finally in ordinary argument between two opponents, when, after a conflict between two partial falsehoods, new truth is discovered, itself only relative, itself assaulted by a counter-truth (antithesis to its thesis), the destruction of each by the other leading once more to a synthesis—a process which continues without end. He called the process dialectical. The notion of struggle and of tension provides precisely that dynamic principle which is required to account for movement in history. Thought is but reality conscious of itself, and its processes the processes of nature in their clearest form. The principle of perpetual absorption and resolu-tion (*Aufhebung*) in an ever higher unity occurs in nature no less than in discursive thought, and demonstrates that its processes are not purposeless, like the mechanical movements postulated by materialism, but lead in the direction of greater and greater perfection. Each major transition is marked by a large-scale revolutionary leap, such as, for example, the destruction of Rome by the barbarians, or the great English or French Revolutions. In each case the Spirit or universal idea advances a step nearer to complete realization, humanity is carried a stage forward, but never strictly in the direction anticipated by either of the two sides engaged in the preliminary conflict, that side being more deeply and more irrationally disappointed, which believed most firmly in its own peculiar ability to force the direction of history.

The new methods of research and interpretation which had suddenly been revealed produced a startling, and even intoxicating, effect on enlightened German society, and to a lesser extent on its cultural dependencies, the Universities of St. Petersburg and Moscow. Hegelianism became the official creed of every man with intellectual pretensions: the new ideas were applied in every sphere of thought and action with an uncontrolled enthusiasm which an age more sceptical of ideas may find it difficult to conceive. Academic studies were entirely transformed: Hegelian logic, Hegelian jurisprudence, Hegelian ethics and aesthetics, Hegelian theology, Hegelian philology, Hegelian historiography, surrounded the student of the humanities wherever he turned. Berlin, where Hegel's last years were spent, was the headquarters of the movement. Patriotism and political and social reaction lifted their heads again. The advance of the doctrine that all men were brothers, that national, racial and social differences were the artificial products of defective education, was arrested by the Hegelian counter-thesis according to which such differences, for all their apparent irrationality, expressing as they do the peculiar genius of a given race or nation, are grounded in some historical necessity. They are needed for the development of the Idea, of which the nation is the incarnation, and cannot be made to vanish overnight by the mere application of reason by individual reformers. Reform must spring from traditional soil; otherwise it is doomed to failure, condemned in advance by the forces of history which move in their own time and at their own pace. To demand freedom from these forces and seek to rise above them, is to wish to escape from one's inevitable historical position, from the society of which one is an integral part, from the complex of relations, public and private, by which every man is made to be what he is, which are the man, are what he is; to wish an escape from this is to wish to lose one's proper nature, a self-contradictory demand, which could be made only by one who does not understand what he is demanding, one whose idea of personal liberty is childishly subjective.

True freedom consists in the discovery of the laws to which, in the particular time and place in which one lives, one is necessarily subject, and in the attempt to make actual those potentialities of one's rational, that is one's law-abiding nature, the realization of which advances the individual and thereby the society to which he 'organically' belongs, and which expresses itself in him and in others like him. When a man in the name of some subjective ideal attempts to destroy a tradition instead of modifying it, he opposes the laws of history, attempts the impossible, and thereby reveals his own irrationality. Such behaviour is condemned, not only because it is necessarily doomed to failure and therefore futile: for situations might occur in which it might be thought to be nobler to perish quixotically than to survive. It is condemned because it is irrational, since the laws of history which it opposes are the laws of the Spirit, which is the ultimate substance of which everything is composed, and are therefore necessarily rational; indeed if they were not, they would not be amenable to human explanation. The Spirit approaches its perfection by gradually attaining the greater self-consciousness with every generation: and the highest point of its development is reached in those who at any time see themselves most clearly in their relation to their universe, that is, in the profoundest philosophers of every epoch. By philosophers are meant the artists and the thinkers, the scientists and the poets, all those sensitive and inquiring spirits who are more acutely and more profoundly conscious than the rest of their society of the stage of development which humanity has reached, of what has been gained in their time and partly by their effort.

The history of philosophy is the history of the growth of this self-awareness, in which the spirit becomes conscious of its own activity; and the history of humanity on this view, is itself nothing other than the story of the progress of the spirit in the process of its growing self-awareness. All history is thus the history of thought, that is, the history of philosophy; which is identical with the philosophy of history, since that is but a name for the awareness of this awareness. The celebrated Hegelian epigram, 'the philosophy of history is the history of philosophy', is, for anyone who accepts the Hegelian metaphysic, not an obscure paradox, but a platitude, quaintly expressed—with the important and peculiar corollary that all true progress is progress of the spirit, since that is the substance of which all else is compounded. Hence the sole method by which those who have the good of society at heart can improve it, is by developing in themselves and in others the power of analysing themselves and their environment, an activity later called criticism, the growth of which is identical with human progress. From this it follows that changes involving physical violence and bloodshed are due solely to the recalcitrance of brute matter, which, as Leibnitz had taught, is itself but thought, at a lower, unconscious level. The revolution instituted by Newton was therefore far more truly a revolution than events which are commonly so called, although it occurred with no bloodshed; all genuine conquest, all true victory is literally, and not in metaphor, gained always in the realm of the Spirit. Thus the French Revolution was in effect over when the philosophers had completed their systems, long before the guillotine began its work.

This doctrine appeared to solve at last the great problem which vexed men's minds throughout the early nineteenth century; the question to which all its leading political theories are so many different answers. The French Revolution had been made in order to secure liberty, equality and fraternity among men; it was the greatest attempt in modern history to embody a wholly new revolutionary ideology in concrete institutions by the violent and successful seizure of power on the part of the ideaologues themselves: and it failed utterly to secure its end. It changed the face of Europe, but its purpose, the establishment of human freedom and equality, was as remote from realization as ever.

What answer was there to those who, bitterly dis-illusioned, fell into cynical apathy, proclaiming the impotence of good over evil, of truth over falsehood, affirming the total inability of mankind to improve its lot by its own efforts. To this problem, with which the social thought of the period of political reaction in Europe is wholly preoccupied, Hegel provided an impressive solution by his doctrine of the inevitable character of the historical process, which involves the predestined failure of any attempt to deflect it by violence, even when the attempt is itself historically necessitated, a view directly opposed to the rival hypo-thesis then being advanced in France by Saint-Simon and Fourier. The problem of social freedom, and of the causes of the failure to attain it, is therefore quite naturally the central subject of all Marx's early writings. His approach to the problem and his solution are in spirit purely Hegelian. His early training and his natural instincts inclined him towards an extreme empiricism: and the modes of thought which belong to this outlook are sometimes visible below the meta-physical accretions beneath which they are for the most part concealed. This emerges most clearly in his passion for exposing irrationalism in every shape and guise; often in his argument he uses the methods of eighteenth-century materialism: but the form in which it is expressed, and the theses it is designed to prove are wholly Hegelian. He was converted to the new outlook in his youth and for many years, despite his vehement attack on the idealist metaphysic, remained a convinced, consistent and admiring follower of the great philosopher.

CHAPTER IV

THE YOUNG HEGELIANS

They [the Germans] will never rise. They would sooner
die than rebel . . . perhaps even a German, when he has been
driven to absolute despair, will cease to argue, but it needs
a colossal amount of unspeakable oppression, insult, injustice
and suffering to reduce him to that state.

MICHAEL BAKUNIN

THE years which Marx spent as a student in the University of Berlin were a period of profound depression
among the radical intelligentsia of Germany. In 1840
a new king from whom much was expected had ascended
the throne of Prussia. Before his accession he had
spoken more than once of a natural alliance of patriotism,
democratic principles and the monarchy; he had spoken
of granting a new constitution; ecstatic references began
to appear in the liberal press to Don Carlos and The
Crowned Romantic. These promises came to less than
nothing. The new monarch was no less reactionary, but
astuter and less bound by routine than his father; the
methods of suppression employed by his police were
more imaginative and more efficient than those in use
in the days of Frederick William III; otherwise his
accession made little difference. There was no sign of
reform, either political or social; the July Revolution in
France, which was greeted with immense enthusiasm
by German radicals, had merely caused Metternich to
set up a central commission to suppress dangerous
thought in all German lands, a measure zealously
welcomed by the Prussian landowning gentry, whose
continued power paralysed every effort towards freedom.

The governing class did all that was in its power to obstruct—it could not entirely suppress—the growing class of industrialists and bankers, which, even in backward and docile Prussia, began to show unmistakable signs of restiveness. Open expression in the Press or at public meetings was unthinkable: the official censorship was far too efficient and too ubiquitous; the Diet was packed with the King's supporters; the gathering feeling of resentment against the landlords and officials, increased by the growing sense of its own strength on the part of the middle class, finally poured itself out in the traditional form of German self-expression, in a flood of words, a philosophy of opposition.

If orthodox Hegelianism was a reactionary movement, the answer of wounded German nationalism to the French attempt to impose its new principle of universal reason upon the world, the secession of its younger members represents an effort to find some progressive interpretation for the formulae of natural development, to detach the Hegelian philosophy from its preoccupation with past history and to identify it with the future, to adapt it to the new social and economic factors which were everywhere coming into being. Both camps, the right and the left, the old, and as they came to be called, the Young Hegelians, based themselves on their founder's famous dictum according to which the real is the rational and the rational is the real; and both agreed that this was to be interpreted as meaning that the true explanation of any phenomenon was equivalent to the demonstration of its necessity, which was tantamount to its rational justification. Nothing could be both evil and necessary, for whatever is real is justified because it is real: *Die Weltgeschichte ist das Weltgericht* (world history is world justice). So much was accepted by both sides. The schism arose over the relative emphasis to be placed on the crucial terms, 'rational' and 'real'.

The conservatives, proclaiming that only the real was rational, declared that the measure of rationality was actuality, that the stage reached by social or personal institutions, as they existed at any given moment, was the sufficient measure of their excellence; so, for example, German culture as Hegel did in fact declare, was a higher, and probably ultimate, synthesis of its pre-decessors, Oriental and Graeco-Roman cultures, from which it presumably followed that the last stage being of necessity the best, the most perfect political framework yet attained by men, consisted of the highest culmination to date of that culture—the Prussian State. To wish to alter it or subvert it was morally bad, because directed against the rational will embodied in it, and in any case futile, because it set itself against a decision already made by history. This is a form of argument with which Marxism later familiarized the world.

The radicals, stressing the converse, protested that only the rational was real. The actual, they insisted, is often full of inconsistencies, anachronisms and blind unreason: it cannot therefore be regarded in any genuine, that is metaphysical, sense, as being real. Basing themselves on numerous texts from Hegel, they pointed out that the master recognized that mere occurrence in space or time was by no means equivalent to being real: the existent might well be a tissue of chaotic institutions, each frustrating the purposes of the other, and so from the metaphysical point of view utterly illusory: their degree of reality was measured by their tendency to form a rational whole, which may necessitate a radical transformation on their part in accordance with the dictates of reason. These are best known to those who have emancipated themselves from the tyranny of the merely actual, and have revealed its inadequacy to its historic role as deduced from a correct interpretation of the character and direction of the past and present. This critical activity against the social institutions of his time, directed by the individual who lifts himself above them, is the noblest function of man, and the more enlightened the critic, the more searching his criticism, the more rapidly will the actual progress towards the real. For, as Hegel had indubitably said, reality is spiritual in character and grows more perfect in the very growth of critical self-consciousness among men. Nor was there any reason to suppose that such progress must be gradual and painless. Citing again the texts undeniably to be found in Hegel, they reminded their opponents that progress was the result of tension between opposites, which grew to a crisis and then burst into open revolution: then and only then did the leap into the next stage occur. These were the laws of development found equally in the obscurest processes of brute nature and the affairs of men and societies.

The plain duty of the philosopher who carries the burdens of civilization on his shoulders is, therefore, to promote such revolution by the special technical skill which he alone commands, that is by intellectual warfare. It is his task to stir men from their indolence and torpor, to sweep away obstructive and useless institutions with the aid of his critical weapons much as the French philosophers had undermined the *ancien régime* by the power of ideas alone. No resort must be had either to physical violence or to the brute force of the masses:

to appeal to the mob, which represents the lowest level of self-consciousness reached by the Spirit among men, is to make use of irrational means, which could only produce irrational consequences: a revolution of ideas will of itself bring about a revolution in practice: *Hinter die Abstraktion stellt sich die Praxis von selbst* (Behind the abstract theory practice appears of its own accord). But since open political pamphleteering was forbidden, the opposition was driven into less direct methods of attack: the first battles against orthodoxy were fought in the field of Christian theology, whose professors had hitherto tolerated, if not encouraged, a philosophy which had shown every disposition to support the existing order. In 1835 David Strauss published a critical life of Jesus written in accordance with the new Hegelian method, in which he rejected some portions of the Gospels as pure invention, regarding others as representing not facts but semi-mythological beliefs entertained in the early Christian communities, and treating the whole subject as an exercise in the critical treatment of a historically important but unreliable text. His book caused an immediate storm not in orthodox circles only, but also among the Young Hegelians, whose most prominent representative, Bruno Bauer, then a lecturer in theology in the University of Berlin, published several attacks upon it from the point of view of an even extremer Hegelianism, wholly denying the historical existence of Jesus, and attempting to explain the Gospels as works of pure imagination, as the literary expression of the 'ideology' prevalent in its time, the highest point reached at this period by the development of the Absolute Idea. The Prussian authorities were not in general interested in sectarian controversies among philosophers, but in this quarrel both sides appeared to hold views subversive of religious, and so, in all likelihood, of political orthodoxy. Hegelianism, which had previously been left in peace as a harmless, and even patriotic, philosophical movement, was suddenly accused of demagogical tendencies. Hegel's greatest opponent, Schelling, then a bitterly reactionary old man, was brought to Berlin in order to refute these doctrines publicly, but his lectures totally failed to produce the desired result. The censorship was tightened, and the Young Hegelians found themselves driven into a position in which they were given the choice of capitulating completely or of moving farther to the political left than the majority wished to go. The only arena where the issue could be still raised were the universities, where a curtailed, but nevertheless genuine, academic freedom continued to survive. The University of Berlin was the chief seat of Hegelianism and it was not long before Marx became immersed in its philosophical politics.

He began his academic career as a student of the faculty of law by attending Savigny's lectures on jurisprudence and those of Gans on criminal law. Savigny, the founder and the greatest theorist of the Historical School of Jurisprudence, and a convinced and rabid anti-liberal, was by far the most distinguished defender of Prussian absolutism in the nineteenth century. He was not a Hegelian in the strict sense, but agreed with the School in rejecting equally the theory of natural rights and of utilitarianism, and interpreted law historically, as a continuous, orderly, traditional development springing from, and justified by, the ideals and character of a given nation in its historical surroundings.

Marx attended Savigny's lectures for two terms with

great regularity, and the immense erudition and power of close historical argument for which the latter was notable was probably Marx's first contact with the new method of historical research, which demanded minute knowledge of facts as a basis for broad general theses. Savigny's chief professional opponent was the professor of criminal law, Eduard Gans, whose effect on Marx was more considerable. Gans was one of Hegel's favourite disciples: he was by birth a Jew, a friend of Heine, and like him a humanitarian radical who did not share his teacher's low opinion of the French enlightenment. His lectures, models, it seems, both of erudition and of courage, were widely attended; his free criticism of legal institutions and methods of legislation in the light of reason, with no trace of mysticism about the past, affected Marx profoundly, and inspired him with a conception of the proper purpose and method of theoretical criticism which he never completely lost.

Under the influence of Gans he saw in jurisprudence the natural field for the application and verification of every type of philosophy of history. Hegelianism at first repelled his naturally positivist intelligence. In a long and intimate letter to his father he described his efforts to construct a rival system; after sleepless nights and disordered days spent in wrestling with the adversary, he fell ill and left Berlin to recuperate. He returned with a sense of failure and frustration, equally unable to work or to rest. His father wrote him a long paternal letter, begging him not to waste his time on barren metaphysical speculation when he had his career to think of. His words fell on deaf ears. Marx resolutely plunged into an exhaustive study of Hegel's work, read night and day, and after three weeks announced his complete conversion. He sealed it by becoming a member of the *Doktorklub* (Graduates' Club), an association of free-thinking university intellectuals, who met in beer cellars, wrote mildly seditious verse, professed violent hatred of the King, the church, the bourgeoisie, and above all argued endlessly on points of Hegelian theology. Here he met, and was soon on terms of intimacy with the leading members of this bohemian group, the brothers Bruno, Edgar and Egbert Bauer, Köppen, a curious figure, one of the earliest students of Tibetan lamaism and the author of a history of the French Terror, Max Stirner who preached an ultra-individualism of his own, and one or two other free spirits (as they called themselves).

He abandoned his legal studies, and became entirely absorbed in philosophy. No other subject seemed to him to possess sufficient contemporary significance: he planned to become a lecturer in philosophy in one of the universities, and together with Bauer to launch a violent atheistic campaign which should put an end to the timorous, half-hearted toying with dangerous doctrines to which the milder radicals confined themselves. It was to take the form of an elaborate hoax, appearing as an anonymous diatribe against Hegel by a pious Lutheran charging him with atheism and subversion of public order and morality, and armed with copious quotations from the original text. This joint work actually appeared and caused some stir; a few reviewers were genuinely taken in, but the authors were discovered, and the episode ended by Bauer's removal from his academic post. As for Marx, he frequented social and literary salons, met the celebrated Bettina von Arnim, the friend of Beethoven and Goethe, who was attracted by his audacity and wit; wrote a conventional philosophical dialogue, and composed a fragment of a Byronic tragedy and several volumes of bad verse, which he dedicated to Jenny von Westphalen, to whom he had in the meantime become secretly engaged. His father, frightened by this intellectual dissipation, wrote letter after letter full of anxious and affectionate advice, begging him to think of the future and prepare himself to be a lawyer or a civil servant. His son sent soothing answers, and continued in his previous mode of life.

He was now twenty-four years of age, an amateur philosopher of no fixed occupation, respected in advanced circles for his erudition and for his powers as an ironical and bitter controversialist. He soon began to be increasingly irritated by the prevailing literary and philosophical style of his friends and allies, an extraordinary compound of pedantry and arrogance, full of obscure paradoxes and laboured epigrams, embedded in elaborate, alliterative, punning prose which can never have been intended to be understood. Marx was to some extent infected by it himself, particularly in his early polemical pieces; yet his prose is compact and luminous in comparison with the mass of neo-Hegelian patter which at this time was let loose upon the German public. Some years later he described the condition of German philosophy at this time: 'According to the reports of our ideologists', he wrote, 'Germany has, during the last decade, undergone a revolution of unexampled proportions . . . a revolution in comparison with which the French Revolution was mere child's play. With unbelievable rapidity one empire was supplanted by another, one mighty hero was struck down by another still bolder and more powerful in the universal chaos. During three years, from 1842 to 1845, Germany went through a cataclysm more violent in character than anything which had happened in any previous century. All this, it is true, took place only in the region of pure thought. For we are dealing with a remarkable phenomenon—the decomposition of the Absolute Spirit.

'When the last spark of life disappeared from its body, its various constituents disintegrated and entered into new combinations and formed new substances. Dealers in philosophy, who had previously made a living by exploiting the Absolute Spirit, now threw themselves avidly on the new combinations. Each busily began to dispose of his share of it. Plainly this could not be done without competition. At first it possessed a solidly commercial, respectable character; but later when the German market became glutted, and the world market, in spite of all efforts, proved incapable of assimilating further goods, the whole business—as usual in Germany —was spoilt by mass production, lowering of quality, adulteration of raw material, forged labels, fictitious deals, financial chicanery, and a credit structure which lacked all real basis. Competition turned into an embittered struggle, which is now represented to us in glowing colours as a revolution of cosmic significance, rich in epoch-making achievements and results.'

This was written in 1846: in 1841 Marx might perhaps have continued to live in this fantastic world, himself taking part in the inflation and mass production of words and concepts, if his circumstances had not suffered a sudden catastrophic change: his father, on whom he financially depended, died, leaving a barely sufficient competence to his widow and youngest children. At the same time, the Prussian Minister of Education finally decided to condemn the Hegelian Left officially, and expelled Bauer from his post. This effectually closed the possibility of an academic career to Marx who was heavily compromised in the Bauer affair, and forced him to look for another occupation. He did not have long to wait. Among his warmest admirers was a certain Moses Hess, a Jewish publicist from Cologne, a sincere and enthusiastic radical, who was even then far in advance of even the Hegelian Left. He had visited Paris and had there met the leading French socialist and communist writers of the day, to whose views he became a passionate convert. Hess, who was a curious blend of ardent traditional Judaism with idealist humanitarianism and Hegelian ideas, preached the primacy of economic over political factors and the impossibility of emancipating mankind without previously liberating the wage-earning proletariat. Its continued slavery, he declared, made all the efforts of intellectuals to establish a new moral world unavailing, since justice cannot exist in a society which tolerates economic inequality. The institution of private property was the source of all evil; men could be freed only by the abolition of both private and national property, which must involve the removal of national frontiers, and the reconstitution of a new international society on a rational, collectivist economic basis. His meeting with Marx overwhelmed him: in a letter to a fellow radical he declared: 'He is the greatest, perhaps the one genuine philosopher now alive and will soon . . . draw the eyes of all Germany . . . Dr. Marx—that is my idol's name— is still very young (about twenty-four at most) and will give medieval religion and politics their *coup de*

grâce. He combines the deepest philosophical seriousness with the most biting wit. Imagine Rousseau,
Voltaire, Holbach, Lessing, Heine and Hegel fused
into one person—I say fused, not thrown together in
a heap—and you have Dr. Marx.'

Marx thought Hess's enthusiasm endearing but
ridiculous, and adopted a patronizing tone which Hess
was at first too amiable to resent. Hess was a middleman of ideas, a fervent missionary rather than an original
thinker, and converted more than one of his contemporaries to communism, among them a young radical
named Friedrich Engels who had not at this time met
Marx. Both learnt from association with him far more
than either was ready to admit in later years, when they
tended to treat Hess, who was not a man of action, as
a harmless but tedious fool. At this time, however, Marx
found him a useful ally, since Hess, who was a tireless
agitator, had managed to persuade a group of liberal
industrialists in the Rhineland to finance the publication
of a radical journal which should contain articles on
political and economic subjects directed against the
reactionary policy of the Berlin government, and in
general sympathy with the needs of the rising bourgeois
class. It was issued at Cologne and was called the
Rheinische Zeitung.

Marx was invited, and eagerly consented, to contribute
regular articles to this journal; ten months later he
became its chief editor. It was his first experience of
practical politics: he conducted his paper with immense
vigour and intolerance: his dictatorial nature asserted
itself early in the venture, and his subordinates were
only too glad to let him do entirely as he pleased, and
write as much of the paper as he wished. From a

mildly liberal paper it rapidly became a vehemently radical one: more violently hostile to the Government than any other German newspaper. It published long and scurrilous attacks on the Prussian censorship, on the Federal Diet, on the landowning class in general: its circulation rose, its fame grew throughout Germany, and the Government was at last forced to take notice of the surprising behaviour of the Rhineland bourgeoisie. The shareholders were, indeed, scarcely less surprised than the authorities, but as the number of subscribers was steadily increasing, and the economic policy pursued by the paper was scrupulously liberal, advocating free trade and the economic unification of Germany, they did not protest. The Prussian authorities, anxious not to irritate the newly annexed western provinces, also refrained from interference. Emboldened by this toleration, Marx intensified the attack and added to the discussion of general political and economic subjects two particular issues over which there was much bitter feeling in the province: the first was the distressed condition of the Moselle vine-growing peasantry; the second, the harsh law punishing thefts by the poor of decayed timber in the neighbouring forests. Marx used both these as texts for a particularly violent indictment of the government of landlords. The Government, after cautiously exploring feeling in the district, decided to apply its power of censorship, and did so with increasing severity. Marx used all his ingenuity to circumvent the censors who were mostly men of limited intelligence, and managed to publish a quantity of thinly veiled democratic and republican propaganda, which more than once led to the reprimand of the censor and his replacement by another and stricter official. The year

1842 was spent in this elaborate game, which might have continued indefinitely if Marx had not inadvertently overstepped the limit. The Russian Government, throughout the nineteenth century, served as the greatest embodiment of obscurantism, barbarism and oppression in Europe, the inexhaustible reservoir whence the reactionaries of other nations were able to draw strength, and consequently became the bugbear of Western liberals of all shades of opinion. It was at this time the dominant partner in the Russo-Prussian alliance, and as such was fiercely attacked by Marx in successive editorial articles: a war against the Russians seemed to him both then and later the best blow that could be struck on behalf of European liberty. The Emperor Nicholas I himself happened to come upon a copy of one of these philippics, and expressed angry surprise to the Prussian Ambassador. A severe note was sent by the Russian Chancellor upbraiding the King of Prussia for the inefficiency of his censors. The Prussian Government, anxious to appease its powerful neighbour, took immediate steps; the *Rheinische Zeitung* was suppressed without warning in April 1843, and Marx was free once more. One year had sufficed to turn him into a brilliant political journalist of notorious views, with a fully developed taste for baiting reactionary governments, a taste which his later career was to give him full opportunity of satisfying.

Meanwhile he had been working with restless energy: he had taught himself French by reading the works of the Paris socialists, Fourier, Proudhon, Dézami, Cabet and Leroux. He read recent French and German history and Machiavelli's *Prince*. For a month he was absorbed in the histories of ancient and modern art in

order to gather evidence to demonstrate the revolutionary and disruptive character of Hegel's fundamental
principles; like the young Russian radicals of this period
he looked upon them as being, in Herzen's phrase, 'The
algebra of revolution'. 'Too frightened to apply them
openly', wrote Herzen, 'in the storm-tossed ocean of
politics, the old philosopher set them afloat in the
tranquil inland lake of aesthetic theory.' Marx's view
of their proper interpretation had lately been affected,
however, by a book which had appeared during that
year—the *Theses on the Hegelian Philosophy*, by Ludwig
Feuerbach, which had been sent him to be reviewed.

Feuerbach is one of those authors, not infrequently
met with in the history of thought, who, mediocrities
themselves, nevertheless happen to provide men of
genius with the sudden spark which sets on fire the
long-accumulated fuel. His own contribution to philosophy is jejune and uninspired, but he was a materialist
at a time when Marx was reacting violently against the
subtleties of the decadent idealism in which he had been
immersed during the past five years. Feuerbach's
simpler style, for all its woodenness and perhaps because
of it, seemed suddenly to open a window into the real
world. The neo-Hegelian scholasticism of the Bauers
and their disciples suddenly seemed to him like a heavy
nightmare which had but lately lifted, and the last
memories of which he was determined to shake off.

Hegel had asserted that the thoughts and acts of
men who belong to the same period of a given culture
are determined by the working in them of an identical
spirit which manifests itself in all the phenomena of
the period. Feuerbach vehemently rejected this.
'What', he inquired in effect, 'is the spirit of an age

or a culture other than a compendious name for the totality of the phenomena which compose it?' To say, therefore, that the phenomena were determined to be what they were by it, was to assert that they were determined by the totality of themselves,—the emptiest and silliest of tautologies. Nor was the case improved, he went on to point out, by substituting for this totality the concept of a pattern, for patterns cannot cause events: a pattern was a form, an attribute of events, which could themselves be caused only by other events. The Greek genius, the Roman character, the spirit of the Renaissance, the spirit of the French Revolution, what were these but abstractions, labels to describe compendiously a given complex of qualities and historical events, general terms invented by men for their own convenience, but in no sense real objective inhabitants of the world, capable of effecting this or that alteration in human affairs. The older view according to which it is the decision and action of individuals that is responsible for change was fundamentally less absurd: for individuals at least exist and act in a sense in which general notions and common names do not. Hegel had rightly stressed the inadequacy of this view because it failed to give an explanation of how the total result emerged from the interplay of a colossal number of individual lives and acts, and showed genius in looking for some single common force responsible for giving a definite direction to these wills, some general law in virtue of which history can be made a systematic account of the progress of whole societies; but in the end he failed to be rational, and ended in an obscure mysticism; for the Hegelian Idea, if it was not a tautological re-formulation of what it is intended to explain, was but a disguised name for the personal God of Christianity, and so lifted the subject beyond the confines of rational discussion.

Feuerbach's next step was to declare that the motive force of history was not spiritual, but the sum of material conditions at any given time which determine the men who lived in them to think and act as they did. Their material distress caused them, however, to seek solace in an immaterial ideal world, where as a reward for the unhappiness of their lives on earth, they would enjoy eternal bliss hereafter. If this illusion was to be exposed, it must be analysed in terms of the material maladjustments which give rise to it. Like Holbach and the author of *L'Homme Machine*, Feuerbach's hatred of transcendentalism often led him to seek for the crudest and simplest explanation in purely physical terms. *Der Mensch ist was er isst* (Man is what he eats) is his own Hegelian caricature of his doctrine: human history is the history of the decisive influence of physical environment on men in society; therefore knowledge of physical laws alone can make Man master of these forces by enabling him to adapt his life consciously to them.

His materialism, and in particular his theory that all 'ideologies' whether religious or secular are often an attempt to provide ideal compensation for real miseries, made a profound impression both on Marx and on Engels, as it later did on Lenin, who read it during his Siberian exile. Feuerbach's treatise is a badly written, unhistorical, naïve book, yet after the absurdities of the unbridled Hegelianism of the thirties, its very *terre à terre* quality must have seemed refreshingly sane. Marx, who was still a liberal and an idealist at this period, was roused by it from his dogmatism. The

Hegelian Idea had turned out to be a meaningless expression: Hegel now seemed to him to have built a specious edifice of words about words and one which it was the duty of his generation, armed with the valuable Hegelian method, to replace by symbols denoting real objects in time and space, in their observable empirical relations to each other. He still believed in the efficacy of the appeal to reason and was opposed to violent revolution. He was a dissident idealist, but an idealist still: a year previously he had obtained a doctor's degree in the University of Jena, with a highly conventional thesis on the contrast between Democritus and Epicurus, both viewed inevitably as precursors of Hegel. In it he defends a materialism far more nebulous than much of what he later himself condemned as typical idealist nonsense.

In April 1843, he married Jenny von Westphalen, against the strongly expressed wishes of the greater part of her family. This hostility only served to increase the passionate loyalty of the serious and profoundly romantic young woman: her existence had been transformed by the revelation to her of a new world by her husband, and she dedicated her whole being to his life and his work. It was an entirely happy marriage. She loved, admired, and trusted him, and was, emotionally and intellectually, entirely dominated by him. He leaned on her unhesitatingly in all times of crisis and disaster, remained all his life proud of her beauty, her birth and her intelligence. The poet Heine, who knew them well in Paris, paid eloquent tribute to her charm and wit. In later years, when they were reduced to penury, she displayed great moral heroism in preserving intact the framework of a family and a household, which alone enabled her husband to continue his work. Together they decided to emigrate to France. He knew that he had an original contribution to make to the agitating questions of the day, and that in Germany it was impossible to speak openly on any serious topic. Nothing held him back: his father was dead, for his family he cared nothing. He had no fixed source of income in Germany. His old associates of Berlin now seemed to him to be a collection of intellectual mountebanks who wished to cover the poverty and confusion of their thought by violent language and scandalous private lives. All his life he detested two phenomena with peculiar passion: disorderly life and histrionic display. It seemed to him that Bohemianism and deliberate flouting of conventions was but inverted Philistinism, emphasizing and paying homage to the very same false values by exaggerated protest against them, and exhibiting therefore the same fundamental vulgarity. Köppen he still respected, but lost all personal touch with him, and formed a new and tepid friendship with Arnold Ruge, a gifted Saxon journalist who edited a radical periodical to which Marx had contributed. Ruge was a pompous and irritable man, a discontented romantic, who after 1848 gradually became transformed into a reactionary nationalist. As a writer he had a wider outlook and surer taste than many of his fellow radicals in Germany, and appreciated the gifts of greater men, such as Marx and Bakunin, with whom he came into contact. He saw no possibility of continuing his journal on German soil in the teeth of the censor and the Saxon police, and decided to establish it in Paris. He invited Marx to assist him in editing a new journal to be called *Deutsch-Französische Jahrbücher*; Marx

accepted the offer with alacrity. 'The atmosphere
here is really too intolerable and asphyxiating', he
wrote to Ruge in the summer of 1843. 'It is not easy
to cringe even for the sake of liberty, armed with pins
instead of a sword: I am tired of this hypocrisy and
stupidity, of the boorishness of officials, I am tired of
having to bow and scrape and invent safe and harmless
phrases. In Germany there is nothing I can do . . .
in Germany one can only be false to oneself.' Marx left
Prussian territory in November 1843, and two days later
arrived in Paris. His reputation had to some extent
preceded him: at that date he was principally thought of
as a liberal journalist with a mordant pen, who was
forced to leave Germany because he had too violently
advocated democratic reform. Two years later he was
known to the police of many lands as an uncompromising
revolutionary communist, a sworn enemy of reformist
liberalism, the notorious leader of a subversive movement with international ramifications. The years
1843-5 are the most decisive in his life: in Paris he
underwent his final intellectual transformation. At the
end of it he had arrived at a clear position personally
and politically: the remainder of his life was devoted to
its development and practical realization.

CHAPTER V

PARIS

The time will come when the sun will shine only upon a world of free men who recognize no master except their reason, when tyrants and slaves, priests, and their stupid or hypocritical tools, will no longer exist except in history or on the stage.

CONDORCET

I

THE social, political and artistic ferment of Paris in the middle of the nineteenth century is a phenomenon without parallel in European history. A remarkable concourse of poets, painters, musicians, writers, reformers and theorists had gathered in the French capital, which, under the comparatively tolerant monarchy of Louis Philippe, provided asylum to exiles and revolutionaries of many lands. Paris had long been notable for wide intellectual hospitality; the thirties and forties were years of profound political reaction in the rest of Europe, and artists and thinkers in growing numbers flocked to the circle of light from the surrounding darkness, finding that in Paris they were neither, as in Berlin, bullied into conformity by the native civilization, nor yet, as in London, left coldly to themselves, clustering in small isolated groups, but were welcomed freely and even enthusiastically, and given free entry into the artistic and social *salons* which had survived the years of monarchist restoration. The intellectual atmosphere in which these men talked and wrote was excited and idealistic. A common mood of passionate protest against the old order, against kings and tyrants, against the

Church and the army, above all against the uncomprehending Philistine masses, slaves and oppressors,
enemies to life and the rights of the free human personality, produced an exhilarating sense of emotional
solidarity, which bound together this tumultuous and
widely heterogeneous society. The emotions were intensely cultivated, individual feelings and beliefs were
expressed in ardent phrases, revolutionary and humanitarian slogans were repeated with fervour by men who
were prepared to stake their lives upon them; it was a
decade during which a richer international traffic in
ideas, theories, personal sentiments, was carried on than
during any previous period; there were alive at this
time, congregated in the same place, attracting, repelling
and transforming each other, men of gifts more varied,
more striking and more articulate than at any time since
the Renaissance. Every year brought new exiles from
the territories of the Emperor and the Czar. Italian,
Polish, Hungarian, Russian, German colonies throve
in the atmosphere of universal sympathy and admiration.
Their members formed international committees, wrote
pamphlets, addressed assemblies, entered conspiracies,
but above all talked and argued ceaselessly in private
houses, in the streets, in cafés, at public banquets; the
mood was exalted and optimistic.

The revolutionary writers and radical politicians were
at the height of their hopes and power, their ideals
not yet killed, nor the revolutionary phrases tarnished
by the débâcle of 1848. Such international solidarity
for the cause of freedom had never before been achieved
in any place: the poets and musicians, the historians
and social theorists felt that they wrote not for themselves but for humanity. In 1830 a victory had been

achieved over the forces of reaction. They continued to
live on its fruits; the suppressed Blanquist conspiracy
of 1839 had been ignored by the majority of romantic
liberals as an obscure *émeute*, yet it was no isolated outbreak: for this seething and nervous artistic activity
took place against a background of hectic financial and
industrial progress accompanied by ruthless corruption,
in which vast sudden fortunes were made and lost
again in colossal bankruptcies. A government of
disillusioned realists was controlled by the new ruling
class of great financiers and railway magnates, large
industrialists who moved in a maze of intrigue and
bribery, in which shady speculators and sordid adventurers controlled the economic destiny of France. The
frequent riots of the industrial workers in the south
indicate a state of turbulent unrest due as much to the
unscrupulous behaviour of particular employers of
labour, as to the industrial revolution which was transforming the country more rapidly and more brutally,
although in a far smaller scale, than in England. Acute
social discontent, together with the universal recognition
of the weakness and dishonesty of the Government,
added to the general sense of crisis and transition, which
made anything seem attainable to one who was sufficiently gifted, unscrupulous and energetic; it fed the
imagination, and produced full-blooded, ambitious
opportunists of the type to be found in the pages of
Balzac, and in Stendhal's unfinished novel, *Lucien
Leeuwen*; while the laxity of the censorship, and the
tolerance exercised by the July monarchy, permitted
that sharp and violent form of political journalism, sometimes rising to noble eloquence, which, at a time when
printed words had a greater power to move, stirred the

intellect and the passions, and served still further to intensify the already electric atmosphere. The memoirs and letters left by poets, painters, novelists, musicians— Musset, Heine, Delacroix, Wagner, Berlioz, Gautier, Herzen, Turgenev, Victor Hugo, George Sand, Liszt— convey something of the enchantment which surrounds those years marked by the acute and conscious sensibility and heightened vitality of a society full of genius, by a preoccupation with self-analysis, morbid indeed, but proud of its novelty and strength, by a sudden freedom from ancient fetters, a new sense of spacious- ness, room in which to move and to create. By 1851 this mood was dead; but a great legend was created, which has survived to our own day, and has made Paris a symbol of revolutionary progress in its own and others' eyes.

Marx had not, however, come to Paris in quest of novel experience. / He was a man of unemotional, even frigid nature, upon whom environment produced little effect, and who rather imposed his own unvarying form on any situation in which he found himself: he dis- trusted all enthusiasm, and in particular one which fed on gallant phrases./ Unlike his compatriot, the poet Heine, or the Russian revolutionaries Herzen and Bakunin, he did not experience that sense of emancipa- tion, which in ecstatic letters they proclaimed that they had found in this centre of all that was most admirable in European civilization. He chose Paris rather than Brussels or some town in Switzerland for the more practical and specific reason that it seemed to him the most convenient place from which to issue the *Deutsch- Französische Jahrbücher*, which was intended as much for the non-German as for the German public. Moreover,

he still wished to find an answer to the question to which
he had found no satisfactory solution either in the
Encyclopaedists, or in Hegel, or in Feuerbach, or in
the mass of political and historical literature which he
consumed so rapidly and impatiently in 1843. What
ultimately was responsible for the failure of the French
Revolution? What fault of theory or of practice made
the Directoire, the Empire, and finally the return of the
Bourbons possible? What errors must be avoided by
those who half a century later still sought to discover
the means of founding a free and just society? Are
there no laws which govern social change, knowledge
of which might have saved the great revolution? The
Encyclopaedists had doubtless grossly over-simplified
human nature by representing it as capable of being
made overnight wholly rational and wholly good by
enlightened education. Nor was the problem brought
nearer solution by the Hegelian answer that the revolution had failed because the Absolute Idea had not
then reached the appropriate stage, since no criterion
of appropriateness to this or that event was given, save
the occurrence of the event itself; nor did the substitution for the orthodox answer of such new formulae as
human self-realization, or embodied reason, or critical
criticism, appear to make it any more concrete, or indeed
to add anything at all.

Faced with the question, Marx acted with characteristic thoroughness: he studied the facts, and read the
historical records of the revolution itself; he also plunged
headlong into the colossal mass of the polemical literature written in France upon this and kindred questions,
and with characteristic thoroughness accomplished both
tasks within a year. His leisure, since his schooldays,

had been mainly spent in reading, but the extent of his appetite in Paris surpassed all limits: as in the days of his conversion to Hegelianism, he read night and day in a kind of frenzy, filling endless notebooks with extracts, and abstracts, and lengthy comments on which he largely drew in his later writings. By the end of 1844 he had made himself familiar with the political and the economic doctrines of the leading French and English thinkers, examined them in the light of his own still semi-orthodox Hegelianism, and finally established his own position by sharply defining his attitude towards these two irreconcilable tendencies. He read principally the economists, beginning with Quesnay and Adam Smith, and ending with Sismondi, Ricardo, Proudhon and their followers. Their lucid, cool, unsentimental style contrasted favourably with the confused emotionalism and rhetoric of the Germans; the combination of practical shrewdness and emphasis on empirical investigation, with bold and ingenious general hypotheses, attracted Marx and strengthened his natural tendency to avoid all forms of romanticism and accept only such naturalistic explanations of phenomena as could be supported by the evidence of scientific observation. The influence of French socialist writers and English economists had begun to dispel the all-enveloping mist of Hegelianism.

He compared the general condition of France with that of his native land and was impressed by its infinitely higher level of intelligence and capacity for political thought: 'in France every class is tinged with political idealism', he wrote in 1843, 'and feels itself a representative of general social needs . . . whereas in Germany, where practical life is unintelligent, and intelligence unpractical, men are driven to protest only by the material necessity, the actual chains themselves . . . but revolutionary energy and self-confidence are not sufficient by themselves to enable a class to be the liberator of society—it must identify another class with the principle of oppression . . . as in France the nobility and priesthood were identified. This dramatic tension is absent in German society . . . there is only one class whose wrongs are not specific but those of the whole of society—the proletariat.' He declares that the Germans are the most backward of western peoples. The past of England and of France is faithfully mirrored in the German present: the real emancipation of the Germans, who stand to more advanced peoples as the proletariat to other classes, will necessarily entail the emancipation of the whole of European society from political and economic oppression.

But if he was impressed by the political realism of those writers, he was no less shocked by their lack of historical sense. This alone, it seemed to him, made possible their easy and shallow eclecticism, the remarkable unconcern with which they introduced modifications and additions into their systems with no apparent intellectual discomfort. Such tolerance seemed to him to show a lack either of seriousness or of integrity. His own view was at all times clear cut and violent, and was deduced from premisses which permitted of no vagueness in the conclusions; such intellectual elasticity, it seemed to him, could be due only to insufficient grasp of the rigorous framework of the historical process. The assumption made by the classical economists that the contemporary categories of political economy held good of all times and all places struck him as particularly absurd. As Engels later put it, 'the economists of the day speak as if Richard Cœur de Lion, had he only known a little economics, might have saved six centuries of bungling, by setting up free trade, instead of wasting his time on the crusades', as if all previous economic systems were so many blundering approximations to capitalism, by the standards of which they must be classified and assessed. Such inability to grasp the fact that every period can be analysed only in terms of concepts and categories peculiar to itself, is responsible for Utopian socialism, for those elaborate schemes which turn out to be so many idealized versions of bourgeois or feudal society with the 'bad' aspects left out; whereas the question to ask is not what one would wish to happen, but what history will permit to happen, which tendencies in the present are destined to develop and which to perish; one must build solely in accordance with the results of this strictly empirical method of investigation.

Nevertheless Marx found the moral taste of these writers sympathetic. They, too, distrusted innate intuitions and appeals to sentiments which transcend logic and empirical observation: they, too, saw in this the last defence of reaction and irrationalism; they, too, were passionately anti-clerical and anti-authoritarian. Many of them held oddly outmoded views about the natural harmony of all human interests, or believed in the capacity of the individual freed from the interference of states and monarchs to secure his own and others' happiness. Such views his Hegelian education had made wholly unacceptable; but in the last resort these men were the enemies of his enemies, ranged on the side of progress, fighters for the advance of reason.

II

If Marx derived from Hegel his view of the historical structure—that is, of the formal relations between the elements of which human history consists, he obtained his knowledge of the elements themselves from Saint-Simon and his disciples, notably Thierry and Mignet. Saint-Simon was a thinker of bold and original views: he was the first writer to assert that the development of economic relationships is the determining factor in history—and to have done this in his day in itself constitutes a sufficient claim to immortality—and further to analyse the historical process as a continuous conflict between economic *classes*, between those who, at any given period, are the possessors of the main economic resources of the community, and those who lack this advantage and come to depend upon the former for their subsistence. According to Saint-Simon, the ruling class is seldom sufficiently able or disinterested to make rational use of its resources, or to institute an order in which those most capable of doing so apply and increase the resources of the community, and seldom flexible enough to adapt itself, and the institutions which it controls, to the new social conditions which its own activity brings about. It therefore tends to pursue a short-sighted and egoistic policy, to form a close caste, accumulate the available wealth in a few hands, and, by means of the prestige and power thus obtained, to reduce the dispossessed majority to social and economic slavery. The unwilling subjects naturally grow restive and devote their lives to the overthrow of the tyrannical minority; this, when the conjunction of circumstances favours them, they eventually succeed in doing. But they grow corrupted by the long years of servitude, and become incapable of conceiving ideals higher than those of their masters, so that when they acquire power, they use it no less irrationally and unjustly than their own late oppressors; in their turn they create a new proletariat, and so at a new level the struggle continues. Human history is the history of such conflicts: due ultimately—as Adam Smith and the eighteenth-century French philosophers would have said—to the blindness of both masters and subjects to the coincidence of the best interests of both under a rational distribution of economic resources. Instead of this the ruling classes attempt to arrest all social change, lead idle and wasteful lives, obstructing economic progress in the form of technical invention which, if only it were properly developed, would, by creating unlimited plenty and distributing it scientifically, swiftly ensure the eternal happiness and prosperity of mankind. Saint-Simon, who was a far better historian than his encyclopaedist predecessors, took a genuinely evolutionary view of human society, and estimated past epochs not in terms of their remoteness from the civilization of the present, but in terms of the adequacy of their institutions to the social and economic needs of their own day; with the result that his account of, for example, the Middle Ages is far more penetrating and sympathetic than that of the majority of his liberal contemporaries. But a social order which responded to genuine needs in its own day may tend to hamper the movements of a later time, becoming a straitjacket the nature of which is deliberately concealed by the classes protected by its existence. The army and the Church, organic elements in the mediaeval hierarchy, are now obsolete survivals, whose functions are performed in modern society by the banker, the industrialist, and the scientist; with the consequence that priests, soldiers, *rentiers*, can survive only as idlers and social parasites, wasting the substance and holding up the advance of the new classes, and must therefore be eliminated. In their place industrious and skilful experts, chosen for their executive ability, must be placed at the head of society: the financiers, engineers, organizers of large, rigorously centralized, industrial and agricultural enterprises, must constitute the government. Finally the laws of inheritance which lead to undeserved inequalities of wealth must be abolished: but on no account must this be extended to private property in general: every man has a right to the fruit of his own personal labour. Like the makers of the Revolution, and Fourier and Proudhon after them, Saint-Simon firmly believed that the ownership of property furnished at the same time the sole incentive to energetic labour and the foundation of private and public morality. Bankers, company promoters, industrialists, inventors must be adequately rewarded by the State in proportion to their efficiency: once the economic life of the society is rationalized by the specialist, the natural virtue of human nature, the natural harmony of the interests of all, will guarantee universal justice, contentment and equality of opportunity for all men alike.

Saint-Simon lived at a time when the last relics of feudalism in Western Europe were finally disappearing before the advance of the bourgeois *entrepreneur* and his new mechanical devices. He had endless faith in the immense possibilities of technical invention and in its naturally beneficent effect on human society: he saw in the rising middle class able and energetic men animated by a sense of justice and disinterested altruism, hampered by the blind hostility of the landowning aristocracy and of the Church, which trembled for their own privileges and possessions, and so became enemies to all justice and to all scientific and moral progress.

This belief was not so naïve then as it may now seem to be. As Marx was himself later to repeat, in the actual moment of struggle for social emergence, the vanguard of the rising class naturally identifies its own cause with the whole mass of oppressed humanity, and feels, and to a certain degree is, the disinterested champion of a new ideal, fighting at the furthest outpost of the progressive front. Saint-Simon was the most eloquent prophet of the rising bourgeoisie in its most generous and idealistic mood: he naturally set the highest value on industry, initiative and capacity for large-scale planning: but he also sharply formulated the theory of the class struggle, little knowing to what application this portion of his doctrine would one day be put. He was himself a landed aristocrat of the eighteenth century, ruined by the Revolution, who had chosen to identify himself with the advancing power, and so to explain and justify the supersession of his own class. His most celebrated ideological rival, Charles Fourier, was a commercial traveller who lived in Paris during those first decades of the new century, when the financiers and industrialists, upon whom Saint Simon had placed all his hopes, so far from effecting social reconciliation, proceeded to sharpen class antagonism by the creation of strongly centralized monopolist concerns. By obtaining control of credit, and employing labour on an unprecedented scale, they created the possibility of mass production and mass distribution of goods, and so competed on unequal terms with the smaller traders and artisans, whom they systematically drove out of the open market, and whose children they absorbed into their factories and mines. The social effect of the Industrial Revolution in France was to create a rift and a state of permanent bitterness between the *grande* and the *petite* bourgeoisie, which dominates the history of that country from that date. Fourier, a typical representative of the ruined class, inveighs bitterly against the illusion that capitalists are the predestined saviours of society. His older contemporary, the Swiss economist Sismondi, had pointed out and defended with an immense mass of historical evidence, at a period when it required something akin to genius to have perceived it, the view that, whereas all previous class struggles occurred as a result of the scarcity of goods in the world, the discovery of new mechanical means of production which would flood the world with excessive plenty, would themselves, unless checked, lead to a class war before which previous conflicts would pale into insignificance. The necessity of marketing the ever-growing produce would lead to a continual competition between the rival capitalists, who would be forced systematically to lower wages and increase the working hours of their employees in order to secure even temporary advantage over a slower rival, which in turn would lead to a series of acute economic crises, ending in social and political chaos, due to the internecine wars between groups of capitalists. Such artificial poverty growing in direct proportion with the increase of goods, above all the monstrous trampling on those very fundamental human rights, to guarantee which the great revolution was made, could only be prevented by State intervention, which must curtail the right of accumulating capital and of the means of production. But whereas Sismondi was a liberal who believed in the possibility of a centrally organized, rationally conducted human society, and confined himself to general recommendations, Fourier distrusted all central authority, and declaring that bureaucratic tyranny is bound to develop, if the government units are too large, proposed that the earth should be divided into small groups which he called phalansteries, each self-governing and federated under larger and larger units; all machinery, land, buildings, natural resources should be owned in common. His vision, an odd blend of eccentricity and genius, at its most apocalyptic moments remains elaborate and precise: a great central electric plant will by its power do all the mechanical labour of the phalanstery: profits should be divided between labour, capital and talent in the strict proportion 5 : 3 : 2, and its members, with no more than a few hours of daily work, will thus be free to occupy themselves with developing their intellectual, moral and artistic faculties to an extent hitherto unprecedented in history. This is at times interrupted by bursts of pure fantasy, such as the prophecy of the emergence in the immediate future of a new race of beasts, not dissimilar in appearance to existing species, but more powerful and more numerous—'anti-lions', 'anti-bears', 'anti-tigers', as friendly and attached to man as their present ancestors are hostile and destructive, and doing much of his work with skill, intelligence and foresight wanting to mere machines. The thesis is at its best at its most destructive. In the intense quality of its indignation, its sense of genuine horror at the wholesale destruction of the life and liberty of the individual by the monstrous régime of financiers and their hirelings, the judges, the soldiers, the administrators, Fourier's indictment is the prototype of all later attacks on the doctrine of the unchecked *laissez-faire*, of the great denunciations of Marx and Carlyle, no less than of the communist, fascist, and Christian protests against the substitution of new forms of privilege for old, and the enslavement of the individual by the very machinery designed to set him free.

The Revolution of 1830, which expelled Charles X and brought Louis Philippe to the throne of France, revived public interest in social questions once more. During the decade which followed, an endless succession of books and pamphlets poured from the presses, attacking the evils of the existing system, and suggesting every kind of remedy from the mildly liberal proposals of Lamartine or Crémieux to the more radical semi-socialist demands of Marrast or Ledru Rollin and the developed State socialism of Louis Blanc, and ending with the drastic programmes of Barbès and Blanqui, who in their journal *L'Homme Libre*, advocated a violent revolution and the abolition of private property. Fourier's disciple Considérant proclaimed the imminent collapse of the existing system of property relations; and well-known socialist writers of the time, Pecqueur, Louis Blanc, Dézami, and the most independent and original figure among them, Proudhon, published their best known attacks on the capitalist order between 1839 and 1842, and were in their turn followed by a host of minor figures who diluted and popularized their doctrines. In 1834 the Catholic priest Lamennais published his Christian socialist *Words of a Believer*, and in 1840 appeared the *Bible of Freedom* by the Abbé Constant, fresh evidence that even in the Church there were men unable to resist the great popular appeal of the new revolutionary theories.

The sensational success of Louis Blanc's *Ten Years*, a brilliant and bitter analysis of the years 1830–40, indicated the trend of opinion. Literary and philosophical communism began to come into fashion: Cabet wrote a highly popular communist utopia called *Voyage to Icaria*. Pierre Leroux preached a mystical egalitarianism to the novelist George Sand, and Heine discussed it with sympathy in his celebrated vignettes of social and literary life in Paris during the July monarchy.

The subsequent fate of these movements is of small importance. The Saint-Simonists, after some years of desultory existence, disappeared as a movement; some of them became highly prosperous railway magnates and *rentiers*, fulfilling at least one aspect of their master's prophecy. The more idealistic Fourierists founded communist settlements in the United States, some of which, like the Oneida community, prospered and attracted leading American thinkers and writers; in the sixties they had considerable influence through their newspaper, the *New York Tribune*.

Marx familiarized himself with these theories, and tested them as best he could, by acquiring knowledge of the details of recent social history from all available sources, from books, from newspapers, by meeting writers and journalists, and by spending his evenings among the small revolutionary groups composed of German journeymen which, under the influence of communist agitators, met to discuss the affairs of their scattered organization and more vaguely the possibility of a revolution in their native country. In conversation with these artisans he discovered something of the needs and hopes of a class, of which a somewhat abstract portrait had been drawn in the works of Saint-Simon and his epigoni. He had given little thought to the precise parts which the *petite bourgeoisie* and the proletariat were to play in the advance of reason and improvement of society. There was in addition the unstable, *déclassé* element, composed of marginal figures, members of odd trades, bohemians, unemployed soldiers, actors, intellectuals, neither masters nor slaves, independent and yet precariously situated on the very edge of the subsistence level, whose existence had hardly been recognized by social historians, still less accounted for or analysed. His interest in the economic writings of the socialists who formed the left wing of the French party of reform turned his attention to these questions. Ruge had commissioned him to write an essay for his periodical on Hegel's *Philosophy of Right*. He wrote it together with an essay on the Jewish question, early in 1844. The essay on the Jews was intended as an answer to Bruno Bauer's articles on this topic. Bauer had declared that the Jews, lagging historically one stage behind the Christians, must be baptized before they could reasonably claim full civil emancipation. Marx in his reply declared that Jews were no longer a religious or racial entity, but a purely economic one, forced into usury and other unattractive professions by the treatment they received from their neighbours, and could, therefore, be emancipated only with the emancipation of the rest of European society; to baptize them would be but to substitute one set of chains for another;

to give them solely political liberties would play into the hands of those liberals who see in these all that any human being can hope, and indeed ought, to possess. It is a dull and shallow composition, but it shows Marx in a typical mood: he was determined that the sarcasms and insults to which some of the notable Jews of his generation, Heine, Lassalle, Disraeli, were all their lives a target, should, so far as he could effect it, never be used to plague him. Consequently he decided to kill the Jewish problem once and for all, so far as he was concerned, declaring it to be an unreal subject, invented as a screen for other more pressing questions: a problem which offered no special difficulty but arose from the general social chaos which demanded to be put in order. He was baptized a Lutheran, and was married to a Gentile: he had once been of assistance to the Jewish community in Cologne: during the greater part of his life he held himself aloof from anything remotely connected with his race, showing open hostility to all its institutions.

The critique of Hegel is more important: the doctrine which it expounds is unlike anything he had published before. In it he had begun, as he himself declared, to settle his account with the idealist philosophy. It was the beginning of a lengthy, laborious, and thorough process which, when it reached its culminating point four years later, proved to have created the foundation of a new movement and a new outlook, and to have grown into a dogmatic faith and a plan of action which dominates the political consciousness of Europe until this day.

III

If what Marx required was a complete plan of action, based on the study of history and observation of the contemporary scene, he must have found himself singularly out of sympathy with the reformers and prophets who gathered in the *salons* and cafés of Paris at the time of his arrival. They were, indeed, more intelligent, more politically influential and more responsible than the café philosophers of Berlin, but to him they seemed either gifted visionaries like Robert Owen, reformist liberals like Ledru Rollin, or, like Mazzini, both at once, unprepared, in the last resort, to do anything for the working class; or else they were sentimental *petit bourgeois* idealists in disguise, sheep in wolves' clothing like Proudhon or Louis Blanc, whose ideals might indeed be at least partially attainable, but whose gradualist, unrevolutionary tactics showed them to be radically mistaken in their estimates of the enemy's strength, and who were, consequently, to be fought all the more assiduously as the internal, often quite unconscious, enemies of the Revolution. Nevertheless he learnt much from them which he did not acknowledge, notably from Louis Blanc, whose book on the organization of labour influenced him in his view of the evolution and correct analysis of industrial society.

He was attracted far more strongly to the party, which, to distinguish itself from the moderates who came to be called socialists, adopted the name of communists. Neither was a party in the modern sense of the word: both consisted of loosely associated groups and individuals. But whereas the former consisted predominantly of intellectuals, the latter was almost entirely composed of factory workers and small artisans, the majority of whom were simple and self-educated men, exasperated by their wrongs and easily converted to the necessity of a revolutionary conspiracy to abolish privilege and private property, a doctrine preached by Babeuf's disciples Blanqui and Barbès, both implicated in the abortive rising of 1839. Marx was impressed in particular by Auguste Blanqui's organizing capacity and by the boldness and violence of his convictions; but he thought him lacking in ideas, and excessively vague as to the steps to be taken after the successful result of the *coup d'état*. He found a similarly irresponsible attitude among the other advocates of violence, the most notable of whom, the itinerant German tailor Weitling and the Russian exile Bakunin, he knew well at this time. Only one among the revolutionaries whom he met in Paris seemed to him to display a genuine understanding of the situation. This was a certain Friedrich Engels, well-to-do young German radical, son of a cotton manufacturer in Barmen. They met in Paris over the publication of economic articles by Engels in Marx's journal. The meeting proved decisive for both; it was the beginning of a remarkable career of friendship and collaboration which lasted during the remainder of their lives.

Engels began life as a radical poet and journalist and ended it, after the death of Marx, as the acknowledged leader of international socialism, which, in his own lifetime, had grown into a world movement. He was a man of solid and robust, but hardly creative mind; a man of exceptional integrity and strength of character, of many varied gifts, but in particular endowed with a remarkable capacity for the rapid assimilation of knowledge.

He possessed a shrewd and lucid intellect and a firm sense of reality which few, if any, among his radical contemporaries could claim. Himself little capable of original discovery, he had an exceptional talent for sifting, assessing and perceiving the practical applicability of the discoveries of others. His knack of writing rapidly and clearly, his unbounded loyalty and patience, made him an ideal ally and collaborator for the inhibited and difficult Marx, whose own writing was often clumsy, overcharged and obscure. In his own lifetime Engels desired no better fate than to live in the light of Marx's teaching, perceiving in him a spring of original genius which gave life and scope to his own peculiar gifts; with him he identified himself and his work, to be rewarded by sharing in his master's immortality. Before they met he had independently arrived at a position not unlike that of Marx, and in later years understood his friend's new, only half articulated, ideas sometimes better than he understood them himself, and clothed them in language more attractive and intelligible to the masses than Marx's often tortuous style. Most important of all, he possessed a quality essential for permanent intercourse with a man of Marx's temperament, a total uncompetitiveness in relation to him, absence of all desire to resist the impact of that powerful personality, to preserve and retain a protected position of his own; on the contrary, he was only too eager to receive his whole intellectual sustenance from Marx unquestioningly, like a devoted pupil, and repaid him by his sanity, his enthusiasm, his vitality, his gaiety and, finally, in the most literal sense, by supplying him with means of livelihood at moments of desperate poverty. Marx, who like many intellectually creative men was himself haunted by a perpetual feeling of insecurity, and was morbidly thin-skinned and jealously suspicious of the least sign of antagonism to his person or his doctrines, required at least one person who understood his outlook, in whom he could confide completely, on whom he could lean as heavily and as often as he wished. In Engels he found a devoted friend and intellectual ally, whose very pedestrianism restored his sense of perspective and his belief in himself and his purpose. Throughout the greater part of his life his actions were performed in the knowledge that this massive and dependable man was always at hand to support the burden in every contingency. For this he paid him with an affection, and a sense of pride in his qualities, which he gave to no one else beside his wife and children.

They met in the autumn of 1844 after Engels had sent him for publication in his periodical a sketch of a critique of the doctrines of the liberal economists. Marx had hitherto vaguely counted Engels among the Berlin intellectuals, an impression which their only previous meeting had failed to dispel. He now wrote to him at once: the result was a meeting in Paris in the course of which the similarity of their views on the fundamental issues became clear to both. Engels, who had been travelling in England and had published a classical description of the condition of the English working class, disliked sentimental socialism of the school of Sismondi even more acutely than Marx. He provided that for which Marx had long been looking, a rich supply of concrete information about the actual state of affairs in a progressive industrial community, to act as the material evidence for the broad historical thesis which was rapidly crystallizing in Marx's mind. Engels, on the other hand, found that Marx gave him what he had been lacking, a solid framework within which to fit his facts, so as to make of them a weapon against the prevalent abstractions upon which, in his opinion, no serious revolutionary philosophy could be based. The effect which the meeting with Marx had upon him must have resembled that which it had made earlier on the more impressionable Hess. It heightened his vitality, clarified his hitherto undeveloped political ideas, provided him with a sense of definite orientation, an ordered view of society within which he could work with the assurance of the concrete, attainable character of the revolutionary goal. This, after aimless wandering in the intricate maze of the young Hegelian movement, must have resembled the beginning of a new life, and, indeed, such for him it proved to be. Their immense correspondence which lasted for forty years was, from the very beginning, at once familiar and businesslike in tone; neither was greatly given to introspection; both were entirely occupied with the movement which they were engaged in creating and which became much the most solid reality of their lives. Upon this firm and reliable foundation was built a unique friendship, free from all trace of possessiveness, patronage or jealousy. Neither ever referred to it without a certain shyness and embarrassment; Engels was conscious of receiving far more than he gave, living in a mental universe created and furnished by Marx out of his own inner resources. When Marx died, he looked upon himself as its appointed guardian, jealously protecting it against all attempts at reform by the reckless and impatient younger generation of socialists.

The two years which Marx passed in Paris were the

first and last occasion in his life on which he met, and
was on terms of friendly intercourse with, men who
were his equals, if not in intelligence, at any rate in
the originality of their personalities and their lives.
After the débâcle of 1848, which broke the spirit of all
but the strongest characters amongst the radicals, deci-
mated them by death, imprisonment and transporation,
and left the majority listless or disillusioned, he with-
drew into an attitude of aggressive isolation, preserving
contact only with men who had proved their personal
loyalty to the cause with which he was identified.
Henceforth Engels was his chief of staff; the rest he
treated openly as subordinates.

The portrait of him which emerges from the memoirs
of those who were his friends at this time, Ruge, Freiligrath, Heine, Annenkov, is that of a bold and energetic
figure, a vehement, eager, contemptuous controversialist, applying to everything his cumbrous and heavy
Hegelian weapons, but, in spite of the clumsiness of
the mechanism, revealing an acute and powerful intellect, the quality of which even those who were most
hostile to him—and there were few prominent radicals
whom he had failed to wound and humiliate in some
fashion—in later years acknowledged freely.

He met and formed a warm friendship with the poet
Heine, whose superb intelligence he valued highly, and
in whom he saw a more genuinely revolutionary poet
than Herwegh or Freiligrath, both, at this time, idolized
by the radical youth of Germany; and he was on good
terms with the circle of Russian liberals, some among
them genuine rebels, others cultivated aristocratic
dilettanti, connoisseurs of curious men and situations.
One of these, an agreeable *flâneur* called Annenkov for

whom Marx conceived a liking, has left a brief description of him at this time: 'Marx belonged to the type of
men who are all energy, force of will and unshakable
conviction. With a thick black mop of hair on his head,
with hairy hands and a crookedly buttoned frock coat, he
had the air of a man used to commanding the respect of
others. His movements were clumsy but self-assured.
His manners defied the accepted conventions of social
intercourse and were haughty and almost contemptuous.
His voice was disagreeably harsh, and he spoke of men
and things in the tone of one who would tolerate no
contradiction, and which seemed to express his own
firm conviction in his mission to sway men's minds and
dictate the laws of their being.' Another, and far more
remarkable member of this circle, was the celebrated
Michael Bakunin, upon whom his meeting with Marx in
Paris at this time had a more lasting effect. Bakunin
had left Russia at approximately the same period as
Marx had left Germany and for much the same reason.
He was at this time an ardent 'critical' Hegelian, a
passionate enemy of Czarism and all absolutist government. He had a generous, extravagant, wildly impulsive
character, a rich, chaotic, unbridled imagination, a
passion for the violent, the immense, the sublime, a
hatred of all discipline and institutionalism, total lack of
all sense of personal property, and, above all, a savage
and overwhelming desire to annihilate the narrow society
of his time, in which, like Gulliver in Lilliput, the human
individual was suffocating for want of room to realize
his faculties to their fullest and noblest extent. His
friend and compatriot Alexander Herzen, who at once
admired him and was intensely irritated by him, said
of him in his memoirs:

'Bakunin was capable of becoming anything—an agitator, a tribune, a preacher, the head of a party, a sect, a heresy. Put him where you like, so long as it always is the most extreme point of a movement, and he will fascinate the masses and sway the destinies of peoples . . . but in Russia this Columbus without America and without a ship, having served, greatly against his will, a year or two in the artillery, and after that another year or so in the Moscow Hegelians, longed desperately to tear himself away from a land where every form of thought was prosecuted as evil-mindedness and independence of judgement or speech was looked upon as an insult to public morality.'

He was a marvellous mob orator, consumed with a genuine hatred of injustice and a burning sense of his mission to rouse mankind to some act of magnificent collective heroism which would set it free for ever; and he exercised a personal fascination over men, blinding them to his irresponsibility, his mendacity, his fundamental weakness, in the overwhelming revolutionary enthusiasm which he communicated. He was not an original thinker, and easily absorbed the views of others; but he was an inspired teacher, and, although his entire creed amounted to no more than a passionate belief in the need for destruction of all authority and the freeing of the oppressed, he built on this alone a movement which lived on long after his death.

Bakunin differed from Marx as poetry differs from prose; the political connexion between them rested on inadequate foundations and was very shortlived. Their main bond was a common hatred of every form of reformism; but it sprang from dissimilar roots. Gradualism to Marx was always a disguised attempt on the part of the ruling class to deflect their enemies' energy into ineffective and harmless channels: a policy which the clearer heads among them knew to be a deliberate stratagem, while the rest were themselves deceived by it, as much taken in as the radical reformers, whose fear of violence was itself a form of unconscious sabotage of their professed ends. Bakunin detested reform because he held that all frontiers limiting personal liberty were intrinsically evil, and all destructive violence, when aimed against authority, was good in itself, inasmuch as it was a fundamental form of creative self-expression. On this ground he was passionately opposed to the aim accepted by both Marx and the reformists, namely the replacement of the *status quo* by a centralized state socialism, since, according to him, this was a new form of tyranny at once meaner and more absolute than the personal and class despotism it was intended to supplant. This attitude had as its emotional basis a temperamental dislike of ordered forms of life in normal civilized society, a discipline taken for granted in the ideas of western democrats, but which to a man of his luxuriant imagination, chaotic habits and hatred of all restraints and barriers, seemed colourless, petty, oppressive and vulgar. An alliance built on an almost complete absence of common aims could not last long: the orderly, rigid, unimpressionable Marx regarded Bakunin as half charlatan, half madman, and his views as absurd and barbarian. He saw in Bakunin's doctrine a development of the wild individualism for which he had already condemned Stirner: but whereas Stirner was an obscure instructor in a High School for girls, a politically ineffective intellectual, neither capable nor ambitious of stirring the masses, Bakunin was a resolute man of action, an adroit and fearless agitator, a magnificent orator, a dangerous megalomaniac consumed by a fanatical desire for power fully equal to that which possessed Marx himself.

Bakunin recorded his view of Marx many years later in one of his political tracts. 'M. Marx', he wrote, 'is by origin a Jew. He unites in himself all the qualities and defects of that gifted race. Nervous, some say, to the point of cowardice, he is immensely malicious, vain, quarrelsome, as intolerant and autocratic as Jehovah, the God of his fathers, and like Him, insanely vindictive.

'There is no lie, no calumny, which he is not capable of using against anyone who has incurred his jealousy or his hatred; he will not stop at the basest intrigue if, in his opinion, it will serve to increase his position, his influence and his power.

'Such are his vices, but he also has many virtues. He is very clever, and widely learned. In about 1840 he was the life and soul of a very remarkable circle of radical Hegelians—Germans whose consistent cynicism left far behind even the most rabid Russian nihilists. Very few men have read so much and, it may be added, have read so intelligently, as M. Marx. . . .

'Like M. Louis Blanc, he is a fanatical state-worshipper —triply so, as a Jew, a German and a Hegelian—but where the former, in place of argument, uses declamatory rhetoric, the latter, as behoves a learned and ponderous German, has embellished this principle with all the tricks and fancies of the Hegelian dialectic, and with all the wealth of his many-sided learning.'

Their mutual hatred became more and more evident as time went on: outwardly friendly relations continued uneasily for some years, saved from complete rupture by the reluctant and apprehensive respect which each had for the formidable qualities of the other. When the conflict ultimately did break out it all but destroyed the work of both, and did incalculable damage to the cause of European socialism.

If Marx treated Bakunin as an equal, he did not conceal his contempt for the other famous agitator, Wilhelm Weitling, whom he met at this time. A tailor by profession, a wandering preacher by calling, this earnest and fearless German visionary was the last and most eloquent descendant of the men who raised peasant revolts in the late Middle Ages, and whose modern representatives, for the most part artisans and journeymen, congregated in secret societies dedicated to the cause of revolution; there were branches in many industrial towns in Germany and abroad, scattered centres of political disaffection round which there accumulated many victims and casualties of the social process, men violently embittered by their wrongs and confused as to their cause and remedy, but united by a common sense of grievance and a common desire to eradicate the system which had destroyed their lives. In his books, *A Poor Sinner's Gospel* and *Guarantees of Harmony and Freedom*, Weitling advocated a class war of the poor against the rich, with open terrorism as its chief weapon; and, in particular, the formation of shock troops out of the most deeply wronged and, therefore, the most abandoned and fearless elements in society—the outlaws and criminals—who would fight desperately to avenge themselves on the class which had dispossessed them, for a new and uncompetitive world in which they would begin new lives. Weitling's belief in the solidarity

of the workers of all lands, his personal stoicism, the
years which he spent in various prisons and, above all,
the fervent evangelical zeal of his writings, attracted
to him many devoted followers among his fellow-
artisans, and made him, for a brief period, a figure of
European magnitude. Marx, who cared nothing for
sincerity when it was misdirected and particularly
disliked itinerant prophets and the vague emotionalism
with which they inevitably infected serious revolutionary work, nevertheless conceded Weitling's importance.
His conception of an open declaration of war against
the ruling class by desperate men who had nothing to
lose and everything to gain, the personal experience
which lay behind his denunciations and moved his
audiences, his emphasis on the economic realities, and
attempt to penetrate the deceptive façade of political
parties and their official programmes, above all his
practical achievement in creating the nucleus of an
international communist party, impressed Marx profoundly. Weitling's detailed doctrines, however, he
treated with open contempt, and, justly believing him
to be muddled, hysterical and a source of confusion in
the party, set himself to expose his ignorance publicly
and lower his prestige in every possible fashion. An
account has been preserved of a meeting in Brussels
in 1846 in the course of which Marx demanded to be
told Weitling's concrete proposals to the working class.
When the latter faltered, and murmured something
about the uselessness of criticism carried on in the
study, far from the suffering world, Marx struck
the table, shouted, 'Ignorance has never yet helped
anyone', and stormed out of the room. They never met
again.

His relation to Proudhon was altogether more complicated. While still in Cologne he had read the book which first made Proudhon's name famous, *What is Property?*, and praised the brilliance of its style and the courage of its author. In 1843 everything appealed to him which revealed a revolutionary spark, anything which sounded clear and resolute and openly advocated the overthrow of the existing system. Soon, however, he became convinced that Proudhon's approach to social problems, for all his declared admiration for Hegel, was ultimately not historical but moral, that his praise and condemnation was directly based on his own absolute ethical standards, and ignored altogether the historical importance of institutions and systems. From this moment he conceived him as merely another French bourgeois moralist, and lost all respect for his person and his doctrines.

At the time of Marx's arrival in Paris, Proudhon was at the height of his reputation. By origin a peasant from Besançon, by profession a typesetter, he was a man of narrow, obstinate, fearless, puritanical character, a typical representative of the French lower middle class which, after playing an active part in the final overthrow of the Bourbons, found it had merely succeeded in changing masters, and that the new government of bankers and large industrialists, from whom Saint-Simon had taught them to expect so much, had merely increased the tempo of their destruction.

The two forces which Proudhon conceived as fatal to social justice and the brotherhood of man were the tendency towards the accumulation of capital which led to the continual increase of inequalities of wealth, and the tendency directly connected with it, which openly united political authority with economic control, and so was designed to secure a growth of a despotic plutocracy under the guise of free liberal institutions. The state became, according to him, an instrument designed to dispossess the majority for the benefit of a small minority, a legalized form of robbery, which systematically deprived the individual of his natural right to property by giving to the rich alone control of social legislation and financial credit, while the *petite bourgeoisie* was helplessly expropriated. Proudhon's best known book, which opens with the statement that all property is theft, has misled many as to his mature views. Early in life he held that all property was misappropriation; later, however, he taught that a minimum of property was required by every man in order to maintain his personal independence, his moral and social dignity: a system, under which this minimum was lost, under whose laws a man could, by a commercial transaction, barter it away, and so, in effect, sell himself into economic slavery to others, was a system which legalized and encouraged theft, theft of the individual's elementary rights without which he had no means of pursuing his proper ends. The principal cause of this process Proudhon perceived in the unchecked economic struggle between individuals, groups, social orders, which necessarily leads to the domination of the ablest and best organized, and of those least restrained by a sense of moral or social duty, over the mass of the community. This represents the triumph of unscrupulous force allied to tactical skill over reason and justice; but for Proudhon, who was not a determinist, there was no historical reason why this situation should continue indefinitely. Competition, the favourite panacea of enlightened thinkers of the previous century, which appeared to nineteenth-century liberals and rationalists in an almost sacred light, as the fullest and richest expression of the individual's strenuous idealism, his triumph over the blind forces of nature and over his own undisciplined appetites, was to Proudhon the greatest of all evils, the perversion of all the faculties towards the unnatural promotion of an acquisitive and, therefore, unjust society, in which the advantage of each depended on, even consisted in, his ability to outwit, defeat, or exterminate the others. The evil was identical with that attacked earlier by Fourier and Sismondi, but it was differently expressed and differently accounted for. Fourier was heir to both the thought and the style of the eighteenth century, and interpreted the calamities of his time as the results of the suppression of reason by the deliberate policy of those who feared its application, the priests, the well born, the rich. Proudhon was to some extent affected by the historicism of his age: he knew no German, but had had Hegelianism poured into him by Bakunin and later by German exiles. Proudhon's attempt to adapt the new theory to his own doctrine with its stress on justice and human rights, led to results which to Marx seemed a crude caricature of Hegelianism.

The method, indeed, by which everything was described in the form of two antithetical conceptions, which made every statement seem at once realistic and paradoxical, suited Proudhon's talent for coining sharp and arresting phrases, his love of epigram, his desire to move, to startle and to provoke. Everything is contradictory; property is theft; to be a citizen is to be deprived of rights; capitalism is at once the despotism of the stronger over the weaker, and of the lesser over the greater; to accumulate wealth is to rob; to abolish it is to undermine the foundations of morality. Proudhon's remedy for this is the suppression of competition and the introduction in its place of a 'mutualist' co-operative system under which limited private property should be permitted, and indeed enforced, but not the accumulation of capital. Whereas competition evokes the worst and most brutal qualities in men, co-operation, besides promoting greater efficiency, moralizes and civilizes them by revealing the true end of communal life. The state may be endowed with certain centralizing functions, but its activity must be severely controlled by the associations by trades, professions, occupations, and again of consumers and producers, under which society would be organized. Organize society into a single economic whole on non-competitive 'mutualist' lines, and the antinomies will be resolved, the good remain, evil disappear. Poverty, unemployment, the frustration of men forced into uncongenial tasks as a result of the class maladjustments of an unplanned society, will disappear and men's better natures will find it possible to assert themselves; for there is no lack of idealism in human nature, but under the existing economic order it is rendered ineffectual or, through misdirection, dangerous. But, for Proudhon, it is useless to preach to the rich; their generous instincts became atrophied long ago. The enlightened prince dreamt of by the encyclopaedists will not be born, being himself a social contradiction. Only the real victims of the system, the small farmers, the small bourgeoisie and the urban proletariat can be appealed to. They alone can alter their own condition, since being at once the most numerous and the most indispensable members of society, they alone have the power to transform it. To them consequently Proudhon addressed himself. He warned the workers against organizing themselves politically, since by imitating the ruling class they will inevitably place themselves at its mercy. The enemy, being more experienced in political tactics, will by bullying, or by financial or social bribes, succeed in luring over the weaker or less astute among the revolutionary leaders, and so render the movement impotent. In any case, even if they were victorious, they would, by acquiring control over, and so preserving the political forms of authoritarian government, give a new lease of life to the very contradiction from which they seek to escape. The workers and small bourgeoisie must therefore seek, by purely economic pressure, to impose their own pattern on the rest of society; this process should be gradual and peaceful. Again and again Proudhon declared that the workers must on no account have recourse to coercion; not even strikes were to be permitted, since this would infringe upon the individual worker's right to the free disposal of his labour.

Proudhon had the unwisdom to submit his book, *La Philosophie de la Misère* (the Philosophy of Poverty) to Marx for criticism. Marx read it in two days and pronounced it fallacious and superficial, but written attractively and with sufficient eloquence and sincerity to mislead the masses. 'To leave error unrefuted', he declared in a similar situation many years later, 'is to encourage intellectual immorality.' For ten workers who might go further, ninety may stop with Proudhon and remain in darkness. He, therefore, determined to destroy it, and with it Proudhon's reputation as a serious thinker, once and for all. In 1847 in answer to *La Philosophie de la Misère* there appeared *La Misère de la Philosophie*, by Dr. Karl Marx, containing the bitterest attack delivered by one thinker upon another since the celebrated polemics of the Renaissance. Marx took immense trouble to demonstrate that Proudhon was totally incapable of abstract thought, a fact which he vainly attempted to conceal by a use of pseudo-Hegelian terminology.

Marx accused Proudhon of radically misunderstanding the Hegelian categories by naïvely interpreting the dialectical conflict as a simple struggle between good and evil, which leads to the fallacy that all that is needed is to remove the evil, and the good will remain. This is the very height of superficiality: to call this or that side of the dialectical conflict good or bad is a sign of unhistorical subjectivism out of place in serious social analysis. Both aspects are equally indispensable for the development of human society. Genuine progress is constituted not by the triumph of one side and the defeat of the other, but by the duel itself which necessarily involves the destruction of both. In so far as Proudhon continually expresses his sympathy for this or that element in the social struggle, he remains, however sincerely he may think himself convinced of the necessity and value of the struggle itself, hopelessly idealist, that is, committed to evaluating objective reality in terms of his own subjective desires and preferences, without reference to the stage of evolution which it has reached. This is followed by a laborious refutation of Proudhon's economic theory, which Marx declared to rest on a fallacious conception of the mechanism of exchange: Proudhon had misunderstood

Ricardo no less profoundly than he had misunderstood
Hegel, and confused the proposition that human labour
determines economic value, with the proposition that it
ought to do so. This leads in its turn to a total mis-
representation of the relation of money to other commodities, which vitiates his entire account of the contemporary economic organization of capitalist society.
The fiercest attack is directed against Proudhon's crypto-
individualism, against his obvious hatred of any tendency
to collective organization, his faith in the sturdy yeoman
farmer and his morality, his belief in the indestructible
value of the institution of private property, in the
sanctity of marriage and of the family, in the absolute
moral and legal authority of its head over his wife and
children; which was indeed the basis of his own life and
was responsible for his deep-seated fear of any form of
violent revolution, of anything likely to destroy the
fundamental forms of life on a small farm, in which his
ancestors were born and bred, and to which, in spite of
his brave revolutionary phrases, he remained immovably
loyal. In effect Marx accused Proudhon of wishing to
remedy the immediate wrongs of the existing system
without destroying the system itself, because, like all
Frenchmen of his class, he was emotionally attached to
it; of not believing, in spite of his veneer of Hegelianism,
that the historical process is either inevitable or irreversible, nor that it advances by revolutionary leaps,
nor yet that the present evils are themselves as
strictly necessitated by the laws of history as the stage
which will one day supersede them. For it is only on the
assumption that such evils are accidental blemishes that
it is plausible to urge their removal by courageous legislation which need not involve the destruction of the social

forms of which they are the historical product. In a rhetorical passage Marx exclaims: 'It is not enough to desire the collapse of these forms, one must know in obedience to what laws they came into being, in order to know how to act within the framework of these laws, since to act against them, whether deliberately or not, in blind ignorance of the causes and character, would be a futile and suicidal act and would, by creating chaos, defeat and demoralize the revolutionary class, and so prolong the existing agony.' This is the criticism which he used against all Utopians who claimed to have a new message for the working class.

Marx was convinced that Proudhon was constitutionally incapable of grasping the truth; that, despite an undoubted gift for telling phrases, he was a fundamentally stupid man; the fact that he was brave and fanatically honest, and attracted a growing body of devoted followers, only made him more dangerous; hence this attempt to annihilate his doctrine and his influence with one tremendous blow. His brutality over-reached itself, however, and created indignant sympathy for its victim. Proudhon's system survived this and many subsequent Marxist onslaughts and its influence increased in the following years.

Proudhon was not primarily an original thinker. He had a gift for absorbing and crystallizing the radical ideas current in his time: he wrote well, sometimes with brilliance, and his eloquence was felt to be genuine by the masses for whom he wrote, springing from wants and ambitions which he had in common with them. The tradition of political non-participation, and of decentralized federalism, of which he was the most eloquent advocate, survives powerfully to this day among

French radicals and socialists, and finds support in the individualist tendency, most pronounced in France and other Latin countries, and natural enough in a land the vast majority of whose inhabitants are small farmers, artisans, professional men, living at a distance from the industrial life of great cities. Proudhonism is the direct ancestor of modern syndicalism. It was affected by Bakunin's anarchism, and half a century later by Sorel's doctrine that, since economic categories were the most fundamental, therefore the units out of which the anti-capitalist force must be constituted should contain men connected not by common convictions,—a mere intellectual superstructure—but by the actual occupations which they pursue, since this is the essential factor which determines their acts. Wielding as its most formidable weapon the threat of disorganizing social life by suspending all vital services by a general strike, it became the most powerful left wing doctrine in many parts of France, Italy and Spain, wherever indeed, industrialism had not gone too far and an agrarian individualist tradition still survived. Wherever central-ization is difficult to achieve, and the tradition of political action is not strong, it still remains the most powerful single opposition to political socialism. Marx, who had an infallible sense of the general direction and political flavour of a movement or a doctrine whatever its ostensible appearance, at once recognized the indi-vidualistic, and therefore for him reactionary, substra-tum of this attitude: and consequently attacked it no less violently than avowed liberalism. *La Misère de la Philosophie* is now, like the specific views which it attacked, largely out of date. But it represents a definite stage in its author's mental development: the first attempt to synthesize his economic, social and political views into the unified body of doctrine, capable of application to every aspect of the social situation, which came to be known as the theory of Historical Materialism.

CHAPTER VI

HISTORICAL MATERIALISM

A certain person once took it into his head that people drown in water only because they are obsessed by the *notion* of weight. If only, he thought, they could rid themselves of this idea, by calling it, for instance, superstitious or religious, they would thereby be saved from all danger of drowning. All his life he fought against the illusion of weight, concerning whose deleterious consequences statistics continually provided him with fresh evidence. This figure is the prototpye of the German revolutionary philosophers of our day.

KARL MARX, *German Ideology*

No formal exposition of Historical Materialism was ever published by Marx himself. It occurs in a fragmentary form in all his early work written during the years 1843–8, and is taken for granted in his later thought. He did not regard it as a new philosophical system so much as a practical method of social and historical analysis, and a basis for political strategy. Later in life he often complained of the use made of it by his followers, some of whom appeared to think that it would save them the labour of historical research, by providing ready-made solutions of all historical research by providing a kind of algebraic 'table', from which, given enough factual data, automatic answers to all historical questions could be mechanically 'read off'. In a letter which, towards the end of his life, he wrote to a Russian correspondent, he gave as an example of dissimilar development despite analogous social conditions the history of the Roman plebs and of the European industrial proletariat. 'When one studies these forms of evolution separately', he wrote, 'and then compares them, one can easily find the clue to this phenomenon; but one will never get there by the universal *passe partout* of particular historico-philosophical theory which explains everything because it explains nothing, the supreme virtue of which consists in being super-historical.'

The most extended statement of the theory occurs in a work which he composed together with Engels in 1846, entitled the *German Ideology*, of which only portions were published before the present century. It is a bizarre compilation, over six hundred pages in length, an amalgam of polemical outbursts against the 'critical' philosophers and exposition of the authors' own views, and contains, among other oddities, an elaborate inquiry into the social significance of Eugène Sue's novel, *Les Mystères de Paris*, a popular thriller of the day which displayed a great deal of specious sympathy with the insulted and the oppressed in the slums of Paris. It contains some effective satire, and passages of considerable critical power, but on the whole it is a verbose and tedious book, dealing with authors and views long dead and justly forgotten.

The framework of the new theory is undeviatingly Hegelian. It recognizes that the history of humanity is a single, non-repetitive process, which obeys discoverable laws. These laws are different from the laws of physics or of chemistry, which being unhistorical, record unvarying conjunctions and successions of interconnected phenomena, whenever or wherever these may repeat themselves; they are similar rather to those of geology or botany, which embody the principles in accordance with which a process of continuous change takes place. Each moment of this process is new in the sense that it possesses new characteristics, or new combinations of known characteristics; but unique and unrepeatable though it is, it nevertheless follows from the immediately preceding state as a result of the similar causes, and in obedience to the same natural laws, as this last state from its own predecessor. But whereas according to Hegel the single substance in the succession of whose states history consists, is the eternal universal Spirit, the internal conflict of whose elements is made concrete, e.g. in the wars of national states, each being the embodiment of a developing Idea which it requires a supersensible intuition to perceive, Marx, following Feuerbach, denounces this as a piece of mysticism on which no knowledge could be founded. For if the world were a metaphysical substance of this type, its behaviour could not be tested by the only reliable method in our power, namely, empirical observation; and an account of it could not, therefore, be verified by the methods of any science. The Hegelian can, of course, without fear of refutation, attribute anything he wishes to the unobservable activity of an impalpable world-substance, much as the believing Christian or deist attributes it to the activity of God, but only at the cost of explaining nothing, of declaring the answer to be an empirically impenetrable mystery. It is this mere translation of ordinary questions into less intelligible language which makes the resultant obscurity look like a genuine answer. To explain the knowable in terms of the unknowable is to take away with one hand what one affects to give with the other. Whatever value such procedure may have, it cannot be regarded as equivalent to a scientific explanation, that is to the classification under a comparatively small number of interrelated laws of the great variety of distinct, *prima facie* unconnected, phenomena. So much for orthodox Hegelianism.

But the solutions of the 'critical' schools of Bauer, Ruge, Stirner, even Feuerbach, are in principle no better. After having so mercilessly unmasked the defects of their master, they thereupon themselves proceeded to fall into far worse illusions: for Bauer's 'spirit of self-criticizing criticism', Ruge's 'progressive human spirit', the 'individual self and its inalienable possessions' apostrophized by Stirner, and even the notion of the human being whose evolution Feuerbach traces, are all generalized abstractions no less empty, no more capable of being appealed to as something beyond the phenomena, as that which causes them, than the equally insubstantial but far more magnificent and imaginative edifice offered by orthodox Hegelianism.

The only possible region in which to look for this principle of historical motion must be one which is open to scientific, that is empirical, inspection: and since the phenomena to be explained are those of social life, the explanation must in some sense reside in the nature of the social environment which forms the context in which men spend their lives, in that network of private and public relationships, of which the individuals form the terms, of which they are, as it were, the focal points, the meeting-places of the diverse strands whose totality Hegel called civil society. Hegel had shown his genius in perceiving that its growth was not a smooth progression, arrested by occasional setbacks, as Saint-Simon and his disciple Comte had taught, but the product of continual tension between opposing forces which guarantee its unceasing forward movement: that the appearance of action and reaction is an illusion caused by the fact that now the first, now the second, of the conflicting tendencies makes itself most violently felt. The progress is discontinuous, for the tension, when it reaches the critical point, precipitates a cataclysm; the increase in quantity of intensity becomes a change of quality; rival forces working below the surface grow and accumulate and burst into the open; the violence of their encounter transforms the medium in which it occurs; ice becomes water and water steam; slaves become serfs and serfs free men; all evolution ends in creative revolution, in nature and society alike. In nature these forces are physical, chemical, biological: in society they are specifically social.

What are the social forces between which the conflict arises? Hegel had declared that they were embodied in nations, each of which represents the development of a specific culture or Idea. Marx, following Saint-Simon and Fourier, and not unaffected perhaps by Sismondi's theory of crisis, replied that these forces were predominantly economic. 'I was led', he wrote twelve years later, 'to the conclusion that legal relations, as well as forms of state, could neither be understood by themselves, nor explained by the so-called general progress of the human mind, but that they are rooted in the material conditions of life which Hegel calls . . . civil society. The anatomy of civil society is to be sought in political economy.' The conflict is always a clash between economically determined classes, a class being defined as a group of persons in a society, whose lives are determined by their possession of a common economic status in that society. The status of an individual is determined by the part which he plays in the process of social production, and this in its turn directly depends upon the character of the productive forces and their degree of development, at any given stage. All individuals act as they do in virtue of the economic relationships in which they in fact stand to the other members of their society, whether they are aware of them or not. The most powerful of these relationships is based, as Saint-Simon taught, on ownership of the means of subsistence: the most pressing of all needs is the need for survival.

Feuerbach for all his crudeness correctly saw that men eat before they reason. The satisfaction of this need can be fully guaranteed only by the control of the means of material production, that is of human strength and skill, of natural resources, of land and water, tools, machines, slaves. There is a natural scarcity of these in the beginning, and they are therefore the objects of violent competition, all the more so because those who secure them are able to control the lives and actions of those who lack them: until they in their turn lose possession of them to their subjects who, grown powerful and cunning in their service, oust them and enslave them, only to be ousted and expropriated by others in their turn. Immense institutions have been created to conserve their possessions in the hands of their present owners, not indeed by deliberate policy, but arising unconsciously out of the general attitude to life of a given society. But whereas Hegel had declared that what gave its specific character to any given society was its national character, the nation being for him the embodiment of a given stage in the development of the world Spirit, for Marx it was the system of economic relations which governed the society in question. In a celebrated passage he summarized this view as follows:

'In the social production which men carry on, they enter into definite relations that are indispensable and independent of their will; these relations of production correspond to a definite stage of development of their material powers of production. The sum total of these productive relations constitutes the economic structure of society—the real foundation on which rise legal and political superstructures, and to which correspond definite forms of social consciousness. The mode of production in material life determines the general character of the social, political and spiritual processes of life. It is not the consciousness of men that determines their existence, but on the contrary their social existence determines their consciousness. At a certain stage of their development, the material forces of production in society come into conflict with the existing relations of production, or—what is but a legal expression for the same thing—with the property relations within which they had been at work before. From forms of development of the productive forces these relations turn into their fetters. Then comes the period of social revolution. With the change of the economic foundation the whole vast superstructure is sooner or later entirely transformed. But in considering such transformations the distinction should always be made between the material transformation of the economic conditions of production, which can be determined with the precision of natural science, and the legal, political, religious, aesthetic or philosophical—in short the ideological forms in which men become conscious of the conflict and fight it out.

'Just as it would be impossible to arrive at a correct

judgement about an individual by noting only his own
view of himself, so it is impossible to judge whole
revolutionary periods by the conscious way in which
they see themselves, for, on the contrary, such consciousness must be explained as the product of the
contradictions of material life, of the conflict between
the forces of social production and their actual relations.
No social order ever disappears before all the productive
forces, for which there is room in it, have developed,
and the new higher relations of production never appear
before the conditions of their existence have matured
in the womb of the old society . . . the problem itself
only arises when the material conditions necessary for
its solution already exist or are at least in the process of
formation.'[1]

Bourgeois society is the last form which these an-
tagonisms take. After its disappearance the conflict will
disappear forever. The pre-historic period will be
completed, the history of the free human individual
will at last begin.

The single operative cause which makes one people
different from another, one set of institutions and beliefs
opposed to another is, so Marx now came to believe,
the economic environment in which it is set, the relationship of the ruling class of possessors to those whom they
exploit, arising from the specific quality of the tension
which persists between them. The fundamental spring
of action in the life of a man, he believed, all the more
powerful for not being recognized by him, is his relationship to the alignment of classes in the economic struggle:
the factor, knowledge of which would enable anyone to
predict successfully a given individual's behaviour, is

[1] *Critique of Political Economy*, trans. by N. I. Stone, pp. 11 ff.

that individual's actual social position—whether he is outside or inside the ruling class, whether his personal welfare depends on its success or failure, whether he is placed in a position to which the preservation of the existing order is or is not essential. Once this is known, his particular personal motives and emotions become comparatively irrelevant to the investigation: he may be egoistic or altruistic, generous or mean, clever or stupid, ambitious or modest. His natural qualities will be harnessed by the circumstances to operate in a similar way whatever their natural tendency. Indeed, it is misleading to speak of 'a natural tendency' or an unalterable 'human nature'. Tendencies may be classified either in accordance with the subjective feeling which they engender, and this is, for purposes of scientific prediction, unimportant, or in accordance with their actual aims, which are socially conditioned. One behaves before one starts to reflect on the reasons for, or the justification of, one's behaviour: and the majority of the members of a community will act in a similar fashion, whatever the subjective motive for which they will appear to themselves to be acting as they do. This is obscured by the fact that in the attempt to convince themselves that their acts are determined by reason or by moral or religious beliefs, men have tended to construct elaborate rationalizations of their behaviour. Nor are these rationalizations wholly powerless to affect action, for, growing into great institutions like moral codes or religious organizations, they often linger on long after the needs, to explain away which they were created, have disappeared. Thus they themselves become part of the objective social situation, part of the external world which modifies the behaviour of individuals, functioning in the same way as the invariant factors, climate, soil, the physical organism, function in their interplay with social institutions.

In the *German Ideology* the claims of the neo-Hegelians are examined one by one and 'awarded' their exact due. The brothers Bruno, Edgar and Egbert Bauer are dealt with briefly and savagely in a section entitled 'The Holy Family'. They are represented as three sordid peddlers of inferior metaphysical wares, who believe that the mere existence of a fastidious critical *élite,* raised by its intellectual gifts above the philistine mob, will itself effect the emancipation of such sections of humanity as are worthy of it. This belief in the power of a frigid detachment from the social and economic struggle to effect a transformation of society is regarded as academicism run mad, an ostrich-like attitude which will be swept away like the rest of the world to which it belongs by the real revolution which could not, by all evidences, now be long in coming. Stirner is treated at greater length. Under the title of St. Max he is pursued through five hundred pages of heavy-handed mockery and insult. Stirner believed that all programmes, ideals, theories, are so many artificially built prisons for the mind and the spirit, means of curbing the will, of concealing from the individual the existence of his own infinite creative powers, and that all systems must therefore be destroyed, not because they are evil, but because they are systems; only when this has been achieved, would man, released from his unnatural fetters, become truly master of himself and attain to his full stature as a human being. This view, which had a great influence on both Nietzsche and Bakunin, is treated as a pathological phenomenon, the agonized cry of a persecuted neurotic, belonging to the province of medicine rather than to that of political theory.

Feuerbach is more gently treated. He wrote more soberly, and had made an honest, if crude, attempt to expose the mystifications of idealism. In the *Eleven Theses on Feuerbach* which he composed during the same period, Marx declared that while Feuerbach had correctly perceived that men are largely the product of circumstances and education, he had not gone on to see that circumstances are themselves altered by the activity of men, and that the educators themselves are children of their age. Feuerbach's doctrine artificially divides society into two parts: the masses which, being helplessly exposed to every influence, must be freed; and the teachers, who contrive somehow to remain immune from the effect of their environment. But the relation of mind and matter, of men and nature, is reciprocal; otherwise history becomes reduced to physics. Feuerbach is praised for showing that religion deludes men by inventing an imaginary world to redress the balance of misery in real life, and thus becomes, in a phrase made celebrated by Marx, the opium of the people: the criticism of religion must therefore be anthropological in character, and take the form of analysing its secular origins. But he is accused of leaving the major task untouched: of seeing that religion is the anodyne to soften the pain caused by the contradictions of the material world, but then failing to see that these contradictions must, in that case, be removed: the revolution which alone can do so must occur not in the superstructure—the world of thought—but in its material substratum, the real world of men and things. 'Philosophers have previously offered various interpretations of the world. Our business is to change it.'

The so-called 'True Socialists', Grün and Hess, fare no better. It is true that they wrote about the actual situation; but, placing ideals before interests in order of importance, they are equally far removed from a clear view of the facts. They believed indeed that the political inequality and the general emotional *malaise* of their generation were both traceable to economic contradictions which could only be removed by the total abolition of private property. But they believed that the technological advance which made this possible was not an end but a means; that action could be justified only by appeal to moral sentiment; that the use of force, however noble the purpose for which it was employed, defeated its own end, since it brutalized both parties in the struggle and made them both incapable of true freedom after the struggle was over. If men were to be freed, it must be by peaceful and civilized means alone, to be effected as rapidly and painlessly as possible, before industrialization had spread so widely as to make class warfare inevitable. Indeed, unless this was done, violence alone would become practicable and this would in the end defeat itself; for a society set up by the sword, even if justice initially were on its side, could not fail to develop into a tyranny of one class over the rest, incompatible with that human equality which true socialism seeks to create. The 'True Socialists' opposed the doctrine of the necessity of open class war on the ground that it blinded the workers to those rights and ideals for the sake of which they fought. Only by treating men as equal from the beginning, by dealing with them as human beings, that is by renouncing force and appealing to the sense of human solidarity, the

sense of justice, and the generous sentiments of mankind, could a lasting harmony of interests be obtained.
Above all, the burden of the proletariat must not be
removed by being shifted on to the shoulders of some
other class. Marx and his party, they maintained,
merely desired to reverse the roles of the existing
classes, to deprive the bourgeoisie of its power only
to ruin and enslave it. But this, besides being morally
unacceptable, would leave the class-war itself in existence and so would fail to reconcile the existing contradiction in the only way possible, by fusing conflicting
interests into one common ideal.

Marx looked upon all this as so much worthless
earnestness. The whole argument, he wearily points
out, rests on the premiss that men, even capitalists, are
amenable to a rational argument, and under suitable
conditions will voluntarily give up the power which they
have acquired by birth, or wealth, or ability, for the sake
of a moral principle, to create a juster world. To Marx
this was the oldest, most familiar, most outworn of all the
rationalist fallacies. He had met it in its worst form in
the belief of his own father and his contemporaries that
in the end reason and moral goodness were bound to
triumph, a theory which had long become discredited
by events during the dark aftermath of the French
Revolution. To preach it now, as if one were still living
in the early eighteenth century, was to be guilty either
of boundless stupidity, or of a cowardly escape into
mere words, or else of deliberate Utopianism, when
what was needed was a scientific examination of the
actual situation. He was careful to point out that he
did not himself fall into the opposite error: he did not
simply contradict this thesis about human nature, and

say that whereas these theorists assumed man to be fundamentally generous and just, he found him rapacious, self-seeking and incapable of disinterested action. That would have been an hypothesis as subjective and irrelevant as that of his opponents. Each was vitiated by the fallacy that men's acts were in the end determined by their moral character, which could be described in comparative isolation from their environment. Marx, true to the method if not to the conclusions of Hegel, maintained that a man's purposes were made what they were by the social, that is economic, situation in which he was in fact placed, and were made so, whether he knew it or not. Whatever his opinions, a man's actions were inevitably guided by his real interests, by the requirements of his material situation; the conscious aims of at any rate the bulk of mankind did not clash with their real interests, although they sometimes appeared disguised as so many independent, objective, disinterested ends, political, moral, aesthetic, emotional, or the like. Most individuals concealed their own dependence on their environment and situation, particularly the class-affiliation, so effectively even from themselves, that they quite sincerely believed that a change of heart would result in a radically different mode of life. This was much the profoundest error made by modern thinkers. It arose partly as a result of protestant individualism which, arising as the 'ideological' counterpart of the growth of freedom of trade and production, taught men to believe that the individual held the means for his happiness in his own hands, that faith and energy were sufficient to secure it, that every man had it in his power to attain to spiritual or material well-being, that for his weakness and misery he ultimately had only himself to blame. Marx maintained against this that liberty of action was severely curtailed by the precise position which the agent occupied on the social map. All notions of right and wrong, justice and injustice, altruism and egoism were beside the point, as referring exclusively to the mental states which, while in themselves quite genuine, were never more than symptoms of the actual condition of their owner. Sometimes when the patient was himself acquainted with the science of pathology he could accurately diagnose his own condition; this is indeed what was meant by genuine insight on the part of a social philosopher. But more frequently the symptom would pose as the only true reality occupying the whole attention of the sufferer. Since the symptoms in this case were mental states, it was this which bred the otherwise inexplicable fallacy that reality was mental or spiritual in character, or that history could be altered by the isolated decisions of unfettered human wills. Principles and causes, unless allied to expressions of real interests, were so many empty phrases; to lead men in their name was to lead them into an impasse, into a state in which their very failure to apprehend their true situation would involve them in chaos and destruction.

To alter the world one must first understand the material with which one deals. The bourgeoisie which wishes not to alter it, but to preserve the *status quo*, acts and thinks in terms of concepts, which, being products of a given stage in its development, themselves served as instruments of its temporary preservation. The proletariat, in whose interest it is to alter it, blindly accepts the entire intellectual paraphernalia of middle-class thought born of middle-class needs and conditions, although there is an utter divergence of interest between the two classes. Phrases about justice or liberty represent something more or less definite when they are uttered by the middle-class liberal, namely, his attitude to his own mode of life, his actual or desired relation to members of other social classes. But they are empty sounds when repeated by the proletarian, since they describe nothing real in his life and only betray his muddled state of mind, the result of the hypnotic power of phrases which, by confusing issues, not only fail to promote, but hinder and sometimes paralyse his power to act. Mutualists, True Socialists, mystical Anarchists, however pure their motives, are thus even more dangerous enemies of the proletariat than the bourgeoisie: for the latter is at least an open enemy whose words and deeds the workers can be taught to distrust: but these others, who proclaim their solidarity with the workers, spread error and delusion in the proletarian camp itself and thus weaken it for the coming struggle. The workers must be made to understand that the modern industrial system, like the feudal system before it, like every other social system, is, so long as the ruling class requires it for its continuance as a class, an iron despotism imposed by the events themselves, from which no individual, whether he be master or slave, can escape. All visionary dreams of human liberty, of a time when men will be able to develop their natural gifts to their fullest extent, living and creating spontaneously, no longer dependent on others for the freedom to do or think as they will, remain an unattainable utopia so long as the fight for control of the means of production continues. It is no longer a struggle strictly for the means of subsistence, for modern inventions and discoveries have abolished

natural scarcity: it is now an artificial scarcity created
by the very struggle for securing new instruments itself,
which necessarily leads to the centralization of power
by the creation of monopolies at one end of the social
scale, and the increase of penury and degradation at
the other; only one remedy—the disappearance of the
class struggle—can achieve the abolition of this widening
gulf. But the essence of a class is to compete with other
classes. Hence this end can be achieved not by creating
equality between classes—a utopian conception—but
by the total abolition of classes themselves.

For Marx, no less than for earlier rationalists, man is
potentially wise, creative and free. If his character has
deteriorated beyond recognition that is due to the long
and brutalizing war in which he and his ancestors have
lived ever since society ceased to be that primitive
communism out of which, according to the current
anthropology, it has developed. Until this state is
reached again, embodying, however, all the conquests,
technological and spiritual, which mankind has won in
the course of its long wandering in the desert, neither
peace nor freedom can be obtained. The French
Revolution was an attempt to bring this about by altering political forms only—which was no more than the
bourgeoisie required, since it already possessed the
economic reality: and, therefore, all it succeeded in
doing (as indeed was its appointed historical task at the
stage of development at which the Great Revolution
occurred) was to establish the bourgeoisie in a dominant
position by finally destroying the corrupt remnant of
an obsolete feudal régime. This task could not but be
continued by Napoleon, whom no one could suspect
of wishing consciously to liberate humanity; whatever

his personal motive for acting as he did, the influence of his historical environment inevitably made him an instrument of social change, and by his agency Europe advanced yet another step towards the realization of its destiny.

The gradual freeing of mankind has pursued a definite irreversible direction: every new epoch is inaugurated by the liberation of a hitherto oppressed class, nor can a class, once it has been destroyed, ever appear again. History does not move backwards or in cyclical movements: all its conquests are final and irrevocable. Most previous ideal constitutions were worthless because they ignored actual laws of historical development and substituted in their place the subjective caprice or imagination of the thinker. A knowledge of these laws is essential to effective political action. The ancient world gave way to the medieval, slavery to feudalism, and feudalism to the industrial bourgeoisie. These transitions occurred not peacefully, but were born in wars and revolutions, for no established order gives way to its successor without a struggle.

And now only one stratum remains submerged below the level of the rest, one class alone remains enslaved, the landless, propertyless proletariat, created by the advance of technology, perpetually assisting classes above itself to shake off the yoke of the common oppressor, always, after the common cause has been won, condemned to be oppressed by its own late allies, the new victorious class, by masters who were themselves but lately slaves. The proletariat is the lowest possible rung of the social scale: there is no class below it; by securing its own emancipation the proletariat will therefore emancipate mankind. Its fight is thus not a fight for the rights of an oppressed section of society: for natural rights are but the ideal aspect of bourgeois attitude to the sanctity of private property: the only real rights are those conferred by history, the right to act the part which is historically imposed upon one's class. The bourgeoisie in this sense has a full right to fight its final battle against the masses, but its task is hopeless: it will necessarily be defeated, as the feudal nobility was defeated in its day. As for the masses, they fight for freedom, not because they choose, but because they must, or rather they choose, because they must: to fight is the condition of their survival; the future belongs to them, and in fighting for it, they, like every rising class, are fighting against a foe doomed to decay, and thereby fighting for the whole of humanity. But whereas all other victories placed in power a class itself doomed to ultimate disappearance, this conflict will be followed by no other, being destined to end the condition of all such struggles by abolishing classes; to abolish the state itself, by dissolving it, hitherto the instrument of a single class, into a free, because classless, society. The proletariat must be made to understand that no real compromise with the enemy is possible: that, while it may conclude temporary alliances with him to defeat some common adversary, it must ultimately turn against him. In backward countries, where the bourgeoisie is itself still fighting for power, the proletariat must throw in its lot with it, asking itself not what the ideals of the bourgeoisie may be, but what it is *compelled* to do in the particular situation: and must adapt its tactics to this. And while history is determined—and the victory will, therefore, be won by the rising class whether any given individual wills it or not—how rapidly this will occur, how efficiently, how far in accordance with the conscious popular will, depends on human initiative, on the degree of understanding of their task by the masses and the courage and efficiency of their leaders.

To make this clear, and to educate the masses for their destiny is, therefore, according to Marx, the whole duty of a contemporary philosopher. But, it has often been asked, how can a moral precept, a command to do this or that, be deduced from the truth of a theory of history? Historical materialism may account for what does in fact occur, but cannot, precisely because it is concerned solely with what is, provide the answer to moral questions, that is, tell us what ought to be. Marx, like Hegel, flatly rejected this distinction. Judgements of fact cannot be sharply distinguished from those of value: all one's judgements are conditioned by practical activity in a given social milieu: one's views as to what one believes to exist and what one wishes to do with it, modify each other. If ethical judgements claim objective validity—and unless they do so, they cannot, according to Marx, be either true or false—they must refer to empirical phenomena and be verifiable by reference to them. He rejected any notion of a non-empirical, specifically moral intuition or moral reason. The only sense in which it is possible to show that something is good or bad, right or wrong, is by demonstrating that it accords or discords with the historical process, assists it or thwarts it, will survive or will inevitably perish. All causes permanently lost are by that very fact made bad and wrong, and indeed this is what constitutes the meaning of these terms. But this is a dangerous empirical criterion, since causes which may appear lost may, in fact, have suffered only a temporary setback, and will in the end prevail.

His view of truth in general derives directly from this position. He is sometimes accused of maintaining that, since a man is wholly determined to think as he does by his social environment, even if some of his statements are objectively true, he cannot know it, being conditioned to think them true by material factors, not by their truth. Marx's statements on this subject are vague to a degree; but in general it may be said that he would have accepted the normal interpretation of what is meant by saying that a theory or a proposition of natural science or of ordinary sense experience is true or false. But he was not interested in this, the most common, type of truth discussed by philosophers. He was concerned with the reasons for which social, moral, historical statements are thought true or false, where arguments between opponents can so obviously not be settled by direct appeal to empirical facts accessible to both. He might have agreed that the bare proposition that Napoleon died in exile would have been accepted as equally true by a bourgeois and a socialist historian. But he would have gone on to say that no true historian confines himself to a list of events and dates: that the plausibility of his account of the past, its claim to be more than a bare chronicle, depends upon his choice of fundamental concepts, his power of emphasis and arrangement, that the very process of selection betrays an inclination to stress this or that event or act as important or trivial, adverse or favourable to human progress good or bad. And this tendency the social origin and environment and class affiliation of the historian affect only too clearly.

This attitude underlies his purely Hegelian view of freedom as identical with the knowledge of the laws of necessity. If you know in which direction the world process is working, you can either identify yourself with it or not; if you do not, if you fight it, you thereby compass your own certain destruction, being necessarily defeated by the forward advance of history. To choose to do so deliberately is to behave irrationally. Only a rational being is truly free to choose between alternatives: where one of these leads to his own irresistible destruction, he cannot choose it freely, because to say that an act is free, as Marx employs the term, is to deny that it is contrary to reason. The bourgeoisie as a class is indeed fated to disappear, but individual members of it may follow reason and save themselves (as Marx might have claimed to have done himself) by leaving it before it finally founders. They can obtain their freedom by discovering the true state of the balance of forces and acting accordingly; freedom thus entails knowledge of historical necessity. Marx's use of words like 'right', or 'free', or 'rational', whenever he does not slip insensibly into ordinary usage, owes its eccentric air to the fact that it derives from his metaphysical views; and therefore diverges widely from that of common speech which is largely intended to record and communicate something scarcely of interest to him—the subjective experience of individuals, their states of mind or of body as revealed by the senses or in self-consciousness.

Such in outline is the theory of history and society which constitutes the metaphysical basis of communism. It is a wide and comprehensive doctrine which derives its structure from Hegel, and its dynamic principle from Saint-Simon, its belief in the primacy of matter from Feuerbach, and its view of the proletariat from the French communist tradition. Nevertheless it is wholly original; the combination of elements does not in this case lead to syncretism, but forms a bold, clear, coherent system with the wide range and the massive architectonic quality which is at once the greatest pride and the fatal defect of all forms of Hegelian thought. But it is not guilty of Hegel's reckless and contemptuous attitude towards the results of the scientific research of his time; on the contrary, it attempts to follow the direction indicated by the empirical sciences, and to incorporate their general results. Marx's practice did not always conform to this theoretical ideal, and that of his followers even less: while not actually distorted, the facts are sometimes made to undergo peculiar transformations in the process of being fitted into the intricate dialectical pattern. It is by no means a wholly empirical theory, since it does not confine itself to the description of the phenomena and the formulation of hypotheses concerning their structure; the doctrine of movement in dialectical opposites is not a hypothesis, liable to be made less or more probable by the evidence of facts, but a metaphysical belief, known to be true by a special, non-empirical, historical intuition: to deny this would be tantamount, according to Marx, to a return to 'vulgar' materialism, which recognizes only those connexions as real for which there is the evidence of the physical senses.

In the sharpness and the clarity with which this theory formulates its questions, in the rigorism of the method by which it searches for the answers, in the combination of attention to detail and power of wide comprehensive generalization, it is without parallel. Even if all its specific conclusions were proved false, its importance in creating a wholly new attitude to social and historical questions, and so opening new avenues of human knowledge, would be unimpaired. The scientific study of economic relations and their bearing on other aspects of the lives of communities and individuals began with the application of Marxist canons of interpretation. Previous thinkers—for example, Vico, Hegel, Saint-Simon—drew up general schemata, but their direct results, as embodied in the gigantic systems of Comte or Spencer, are at once too abstract and too vague, and as forgotten in our day as they deserve to be. The true father of modern economic history, and, indeed, of modern sociology, in so far as any one man may claim that title, is Karl Marx. If to have turned into truisms what had previously been paradoxes is a mark of genius, Marx was richly endowed with it. His achievements in this sphere are necessarily forgotten in proportion as their effects have become part of the permanent background of civilized thought.

CHAPTER VII

1848

Gegen Demokraten Helfen nur Soldaten.
(Against democrats, only soldiers help.)

Prussian Song.

Liberty, Equality, Fraternity . . . when what this republic really means is Infantry, Cavalry, Artillery. . . .

KARL MARX, *Eighteenth Brumaire of Louis Bonaparte.*

MARX was expelled from Paris in the beginning of 1845 by the Guizot government, as a result of representations from Prussia, which had demanded the suppression of the socialist *Vorwärts* in which offensive comments had appeared concerning the character of the reigning Prussian king. The order of expulsion was originally intended to apply to the entire group, including Heine, Bakunin, Ruge and several other lesser foreign exiles. Ruge, being a Saxon citizen, was left unmolested; the French government itself did not venture to press the order against Heine, a figure of European fame, then at the height of his powers and influence. Bakunin and Marx were duly expelled in spite of vigorous protests in the radical press. Bakunin went to Switzerland; Marx, with his wife and one-year-old daughter Jenny, to Brussels where shortly afterwards he was joined by Engels who had returned from England for this purpose. In Brussels he lost no time in establishing contact with the various German communist workers' organizations which contained members of the dissolved League of the Just, an international society of proletarian revolutionaries with a vague, but violent, programme, influenced by Weitling;

it had branches in various European cities. He entered into relations with Belgian socialists and radicals, carried on an active correspondence with members of similar bodies in other countries, and established regular machinery for the exchange of political information, but the chief sphere of his activity lay among the German workmen in Brussels itself. To these he attempted by means of lectures, and of articles in their organ, the *Brüsseler Zeitung*, to explain their proper part in the coming revolution, which he, like the majority of European radicals, believed to be imminent.

As soon as he concluded that the establishment of communism could only be achieved by an armed rising of the proletariat, his entire existence turned into an attempt to organize and discipline it for its task. His personal history which up to this point can be regarded as a series of episodes in the life of an individual, now becomes inseparable from the general history of socialism in Europe. An account of one is necessarily to some degree an account of the other. Attempts to distinguish the part which Marx played in directing the movement from the movement itself obscure the history of both. The task of preparing the workers for the revolution was for him a scientific task, a routine occupation, something to be performed as solidly and efficiently as possible, and not a direct means of personal self-expression. The external circumstances of his life are therefore as monotonous as those of any other devoted expert, as those of Darwin or Pasteur, and offer the sharpest possible contrast to the restless, emotionally involved, lives of the other revolutionaries of his time.

The middle decades of the nineteenth century form a period in which an enormous premium was placed on sensibility. What had begun by being the isolated experience of exceptional individuals, of Byron and Shelley, Rousseau and Chateaubriand, Schiller and Jean Paul, by insensible degrees became part of the general attitude of European society. For the first time a whole generation became fascinated by the personal experience of men and women, as opposed to the external world composed of interplay of the lives of whole groups or societies. This tendency obtained public expression in the lives and doctrines of the great democratic revolutionaries, and in the passionate adoration with which they were regarded by their followers: Mazzini, Kossuth, Garibaldi, Bakunin, Lassalle, were admired not only as heroic fighters for freedom, but for their romantic, poetical properties as individuals. Their achievements were looked upon as the expression of profound inner experience, the intensity of which gave their words and gestures a moving personal quality wholly different from the austerely impersonal heroism of the men of 1789, a quality which constitutes the distinguishing characteristic, the peculiar Hegelian essence of the age. Karl Marx belonged in spirit to an earlier or a later generation; but certainly not to his own time. He lacked psychological insight, and poverty and hard work did not increase his emotional receptiveness; this extreme blindness to the experience and character of persons outside his immediate range made his intercourse with the outside world seem singularly boorish; he had had a brief sentimental period as a student in Berlin: this was now over and done with. He looked upon moral or emotional suffering, and spiritual crises, as so much bourgeois self-indulgence unpardonable in time of war: like Lenin after him, he had nothing but contempt for those who, during the heat of the battle, while the enemy gained one position after another, were preoccupied with the state of their own souls.

He set to work to create an international revolutionary organization. He received the warmest response from London, from a society called the German Workers' Educational Association, headed by a small group of exiled artisans, whose revolutionary temper was beyond suspicion: the type-setter Schapper, the watch-maker Moll and the cobbler Bauer were his first reliable political allies. They had affiliated their society to a federation called the Communist League which succeeded the dissolved League of the Just. He met them in the course of a journey to England with Engels, and found them men after his own heart, determined, capable and energetic. They looked on him with considerable suspicion as a journalist and an intellectual: and their relations for some years preserved a severely impersonal and business-like character. It was an association for immediate practical ends, but this he approved. Under his guidance, the Communist League grew fast and began to embrace groups of radical workers, scattered for the most part in the industrial areas in Germany, with a sprinkling of army officers and professional men. Engels wrote glowing reports of the increase in their numbers and their revolutionary zeal in his own native province. For the first time Marx found himself in the position which he had long desired, the organizer and leader of an active and expanding revolutionary party. Bakunin, who had in his turn arrived in Brussels, and was on equally good terms with the foreign radicals and members of the local aristocracy, complained that Marx preferred the society of artisans and workmen to that of intelligent people, and was spoiling good and simple men by filling their heads with abstract theories and obscure economic doctrines, which they did not begin to understand, and which only made them intolerably conceited. He saw no point in lecturing to, and organizing small groups of ill-educated and hopelessly limited German artisans, who understood little of what was so elaborately expounded to them, drab, underfed creatures who could not conceivably turn the scale in any decisive conflict. Marx's attack on Proudhon still further estranged them; Proudhon was an intimate friend and, in Hegelian matters, a disciple of Bakunin; and the attack was aimed no less at Bakunin's own habit of indulging in vague and exuberant eloquence in place of detailed political analysis.

The events of 1848 altered the view of both on the technique of the coming revolution, but in precisely opposed directions. Bakunin in later years turned to secret terrorist groups, Marx to the foundation of an open official revolutionary party proceeding by recognized political methods. He set himself to destroy the tendency to rhetoric and vagueness among the Germans, nor was he wholly unsuccessful, as may be seen in the efficient and disciplined behaviour of the members of his organization in Germany during the two revolutionary years and after.

In 1847 the London centre of the Communist League showed its confidence in him by commissioning him to compose a document containing a definitive statement of its beliefs and aims. He eagerly embraced this opportunity for an explicit summary of the new doctrine which had lately assumed its final shape in his head.

He delivered it into their hands early in 1848. It was published a few weeks before the outbreak of the Paris revolution under the title of *The Manifesto of the Communist Party*.

Engels wrote the first draft in the form of questions and answers, but since this was not thought sufficiently forcible, Marx completely re-wrote it. According to Engels the result was an original work which owed hardly anything to his own hand; but he was excessively modest wherever their collaboration was concerned, so that it is virtually impossible to say how great a share he had in its composition. The result is very nearly a work of genius. No other modern political movement or cause can claim to have produced anything comparable with it in eloquence or power. It is a document of prodigious dramatic force; in form it is an edifice of bold and arresting historical generalizations, mounting to a denunciation of the existing order in the name of the avenging forces of the future, much of it written in prose which has the lyrical quality of a great revolutionary hymn, whose effect overwhelming even now, was probably greater at the time. It opens with a menacing phrase which reveals its tone and its intention: 'A spectre is wandering over Europe to-day—the spectre of communism. All the forces of Europe have united to exorcise it: the Pope and the Czar, Metternich and Guizot, French radicals and German policemen . . . it is recognized as a real force by all the European powers.' It proceeds as a succession of interconnected theses which are developed and brilliantly embroidered, and ends with a famous and magnificent invocation addressed to the workers of the world.

The first of these theses is contained in the opening

sentence of the first section: 'The history of all previous
society is the history of class struggles.' At all periods
within recorded memory mankind has been divided
into exploiter and exploited, master and slave, patrician
and plebeian, and in our day proletarian and capitalist.
The immense development of discovery and invention
has transformed the economic system of modern human
society: guilds have given way to local manufacture,
and this in its turn to great industrial enterprises. Each
stage in this expansion is accompanied by political and
cultural forms peculiar to itself. The structure of the
modern State reflects the domination of the bourgeoisie
—it is in effect a committee for managing the affairs of
the bourgeois class as a whole. The bourgeoisie fulfilled
a highly revolutionary role in its day; it overthrew the
feudal order and in so doing destroyed the old, picturesque, patriarchal, relations which connected a man
to his 'natural masters' and left only one real relation
between them—the cash nexus, naked self-interest. It
has turned personal dignity into a negotiable commodity, to be bought and sold; in place of ancient
liberties, secured by writs and charters, is has created
freedom of trade; for exploitation disguised by religious
and political masks, it has substituted exploitation,
direct, cynical and unashamed. It has turned professions formerly thought honourable, as being forms of
service to the community, into mere hired labour:
acquisitive in its aims, it has degraded every form of life.
This was achieved by calling immense new natural
resources into existence: the feudal framework could not
contain the new development, and was split asunder.
Now the process has repeated itself. The frequent
economic crises due to over-production are a symptom

of the fact that capitalism can in its turn no longer
control its own resources. When a social order is forced
to destroy its own products, to prevent its own faculties
from expanding too rapidly and too far, that is a
certain sign of its approaching bankruptcy and doom.
The bourgeois order has created the proletariat which
is at once its heir and its executioner. It has succeeded
in destroying the power of all other rival forms of organization, the aristocracy, the small artisans and leaders,
but the proletariat it cannot destroy, for it is necessary
to its own existence, is an organic part of its system, and
constitutes the great army of the dispossessed, whom in
the very act of exploiting it inevitably disciplines and
organizes. The more international capitalism becomes
—and as it expands, it inevitably grows more so—the
wider and more international the scale on which it
automatically organizes the workers, whose union and
solidarity will eventually overthrow it. The international
of capitalism breeds inevitably, as its own necessary
complement, the international of the working class.
This dialectical process is inexorable, and no power can
arrest it or control it. Hence it is futile to attempt to
restore the old medieval idyll, to build utopian schemes on
a nostalgic desire to return to the past, for which the
ideologists of peasants, artisans, small traders so ardently
long. The past is gone, the classes which belonged
to it have long been decisively defeated by the force
of history; their hostility toward the bourgeoisie, often
falsely called socialism, is a reactionary attitude, a
futile attempt to reverse the advance of human evolution.
Their only hope of triumph over the enemy lies in
abandonment of their independent existence and fusion
with the proletariat, whose growth corrodes the

bourgeoisie from within; for the increases of crises and of unemployment forces the bourgeoisie to exhaust itself in feeding its servants instead of feeding on them, which is its natural function.

From attack the Manifesto passes to defence. The enemies of socialism declare that the abolition of private property will destroy liberty and subvert the foundations of religion, morality and culture. This is admitted. But the values which it will thus destroy will be only those which are bound up with the old order—bourgeois liberty and bourgeois culture, whose appearance of absolute validity for all times and places is an illusion due solely to their function as a weapon in class struggle. True personal freedom is possession of the power of independent action, of which the artisan, the small trader, the peasant, has long been deprived by capitalism. As for culture, 'the culture the loss of which is lamented is, for the enormous majority, a mere training to act as a machine'. With the total abolition of the class struggle these illusory ideals will necessarily vanish and be succeeded by the new and wider form of life founded upon a classless society. To mourn their loss is to lament the disappearance of an old familiar ailment.

The revolution must differ in differing circumstances, but its first measures everywhere must be the nationalization of land, credit, transport, the abolition of rights of inheritance, the increase of taxation, the intensification of production, the destruction of the barriers between town and country, the introduction of compulsory work and of free education for all. Only then can serious social reconstruction begin. The rest of the Manifesto exposes and refutes various forms of pseudo-socialism—the attempts of various enemies of the bourgeoisie, the aristocracy, or the Church, to gain the proletariat to its cause by specious pretence of common interest. Into this category enters the ruined *petite bourgeoisie*, whose writers, adept as they are at exposing the chaos of capitalist production, the pauperization and degradation caused by the introduction of machinery, the monstrous inequalities of wealth, offer remedies which, being conceived in obsolete terms, are utopian. Even this cannot be said of the German 'True Socialists', who by translating French platitudes into the language of Hegelianism, produce a meaningless collection of nonsense phrases which cannot long deceive the world. As for Proudhon, Fourier or Owen, their followers draw up schemes to save the bourgeoisie, as if the proletariat did not exist, or else could be drawn upwards into capitalist ranks, leaving only exploiters and no exploited. This endless variety of views represents the desperate plight of the bourgeoisie unable or unwilling to face its own impending death, concentrating upon vain efforts to survive under the guise of a vague and opportunist socialism. As for the communists, they are not a party or a sect, but the self-conscious vanguard of the proletariat itself, obsessed by no mere theoretical ends, but seeking to fulfil their historical destiny. They do not conceal their aims. They openly declare that these can be gained only when the entire social order is overthrown by force of arms, and they themselves seize all political and economic power. The Manifesto ends with the celebrated words : 'The workers have nothing to lose but their chains. They have a world to win. Workers of all lands, unite!'

No summary can convey the quality of its opening or its closing pages. As an instrument of destructive propaganda it has no equal anywhere; its effect upon succeeding generations is unparalleled outside religious history; had its author written nothing else, it would have ensured his lasting fame. Its most immediate effect, however, was upon his own fortunes. The Belgian Government, which behaved with considerable tolerance to political exiles, could not overlook this formidable publication, and brusquely expelled him and his family from its territory. On the next day the long expected revolution broke out in Paris. Flocon, a radical member of the new French Government, in a flattering letter, invited Marx to return to the revolutionary city. He set off immediately and arrived a day later.

He found the city in a state of universal and uncritical enthusiasm. The barriers had fallen once more, this time it seemed for ever. The king had fled, declaring that he had been driven out by moral forces, a new Government had been appointed containing representatives of all the friends of humanity and progress: the great physicist Arago and the poet Lamartine received portfolios, the workers were represented by Louis Blanc and Albert. Lamartine composed an eloquent manifesto which was read, quoted, declaimed everywhere. The streets were filled with an immense singing, cheering throng of democrats of all hues and nationalities. The opposition showed no sign of life. The Church published a manifesto in which it asserted that Christianity was not inimical to individual liberty, that on the contrary it was its natural ally and defender; its kingdom was not of this world, and consequently such support as it had been accused of giving to the reaction, sprang neither from its principles nor from its historical

position in European society, and could be radically
modified without doing violence to the essence of its
teaching. These announcements were received with
enthusiasm and credulity. The German exiles vied
with the Poles and the Italians in their predictions of the
imminent and universal collapse of the reaction, and
of the immediate appearance on its ruins of a new moral
world. News presently arrived that Naples had revolted;
and after it Milan, Rome, Venice and other Italian
cities. Berlin, Vienna, and Budapest had risen in arms.
Europe was ablaze at last. Excitement among the
Germans in Paris rose to fever pitch. To support the
insurgent republicans a German Legion was formed,
which the poet Georg Herwegh and a Prussian communist ex-soldier named Willich were to lead. It was
to start at once. The French Government, not unwilling,
perhaps, to see so many foreign agitators leave its soil,
encouraged the project. Engels was greatly attracted
by the scheme and would almost certainly have enlisted,
but was dissuaded by Marx, who viewed the proceeding
with the greatest mistrust and hostility. He saw no sign
of any large-scale revolt of the German masses: here
and there autocratic governments were overthrown, and
the princes were forced to promise constitutions and
appoint mildly liberal governments, but the Prussian
army was still largely loyal to the king, while the democrats were scattered, badly led, and unable to reach
agreement among themselves on vital points. The
elected popular congress which met in Frankfurt to
decide the future government of Germany was a failure
from the first, and the sudden appearance of a legion of
untrained *émigré* intellectuals on German soil appeared
to Marx a needless waste of revolutionary energy, likely

to have a ludicrous or a pitiful end, and to be followed by a paralysing mood of shame and disillusionment. Consequently, Marx opposed the formation of the legion, took no interest in it after it had left Paris for its inevitable defeat by the royal army, and went to Cologne to see what could be done by propaganda in his native Rhineland. He was there largely instrumental in persuading a group of liberal industrialists and communist sympathizers to found a new *Rheinische Zeitung*, in succession to the journal of that name which had been suppressed five years before, and to appoint him its editor. Cologne was then the scene of an uneasy balance of power between the local democrats, who controlled the local militia, and a garrison under orders from Berlin. Acting in the name of the Communist League, Marx sent his agents to agitate among the German industrial masses, and used their reports as the material for his leading articles. There was at this time no formal censorship in the Rhineland, and his inflammatory words reached an ever-widening public. The *Neue Rheinische Zeitung* was well informed, and alone in the left-wing press possessed a clear policy of its own. Its circulation increased rapidly and it began to be widely read in other German provinces.

Marx had come armed with a complete political and economic plan of action founded on the solid theoretical basis which he had built carefully during the preceding years. He advocated a conditional alliance between the workers and the radical bourgeoisie for the immediate purpose of overthrowing a reactionary government, declaring that whereas the French had freed themselves from the yoke of feudalism in 1789, and were by this enabled to take the next step forward in 1848, the

Germans had so far achieved their revolutions in the region of pure thought alone; as thinkers they had far outstripped the French in the radicalism of their sentiments: politically they still inhabited the eighteenth century. The most backward of western nations, they thus had two stages to achieve before they could hope to attain to that of developed industrialism, thenceforth to march in step with the neighbouring democracies. The dialectical movement of history permits no leaps, and the representatives of the proletariat did ill to overlook the claims of the bourgeoisie which, in working for its own emancipation, was furthering the general cause, and was economically and politically far better organized and capable of ruling than the ignorant, scattered, badly organized masses of the working class. Hence the proper step for the workers was to conclude an alliance with their fellow victims among the middle and lower middle class and then, after the victory, to seek to control, and if necessary, obstruct the work of their new allies (who by this time would doubtless be anxious to end their compromising association) by the sheer weight of their numbers and economic power. He opposed the Cologne democrats, Anneke and Gottschalk, who advocated absolute abstention from such naked opportunism and indeed from all political action as likely to compromise and weaken the pure proletarian cause. This seemed to him a typically German blindness to the true balance of forces. He demanded direct intervention and the sending of delegates to Frankfurt, as the only effective practical course. Political aloofness seemed to him the height of tactical folly, since it was likely to leave the workers isolated, and at the mercy of the victorious class. In foreign policy he was a pronounced pan-German and a rabid Russophobe. Russia had for many years occupied the same position in relation to the forces of democracy and progress and evoked the same emotional reaction as the fascist powers in the present day. It was hated and feared by democrats of all persuasions as the great champion of reaction, able and willing to crush all attempts at liberty within and without its borders.

As in 1842, Marx demanded an immediate war with Russia, because no attempt at democratic revolution could succeed in Germany in view of the certainty of Russian intervention, and as a means of welding the German principalities into a united democratic whole in opposition to a power whose entire influence was ranged on the side of the dynastic element in European politics; perhaps also in order to aid those scattered revolutionary forces within Russia itself to the existence of which Bakunin used to make constant mysterious references. Marx was prepared to sacrifice many other considerations to the ends of German unity—since in its disunion he, no less than Hegel and Bismarck, saw the cause at once of its weakness, its inefficiency and its political backwardness. He was neither a romantic, nor a nationalist, and regarded small nations as so many obsolete survivals impeding social and economic progress. He therefore acted quite consistently in publicly approving the unwarranted German invasion of the Danish province of Schleswig-Holstein; an act, the open support of which by most of the leading German democrats, caused considerable embarrassment to their allies among the liberals and constitutionalists of other lands.

He denounced the succession of short-lived liberal

Prussian governments which, easily and, it seemed to him, almost with relief, allowed power to slip from their grasp back into that of the king and his party. There were furious outbursts against 'empty chatter' and of 'parliamentary cretinism' in Frankfurt, which ended in a storm of indignation hardly paralleled in *Das Kapital* itself. He did not either then or later despair of the ultimate outcome of the conflict, but his conception of the revolutionary tactics, and his view of the intelligence and reliability of the masses and their leaders, changed violently: he declared their own incurable stupidity to be a greater obstacle to their progress than capitalism itself. His own policy, as it turned out, proved as impracticable as that of the intransigent radicals whom he denounced. In his subsequent analysis he attributed the disastrous result of the revolution to the weakness of the bourgeoisie, the ineffectiveness of the parliamentary liberals, but principally to the political blindness of the infinitely gullible masses, obstinately loyal to the agents of their own worst enemy, who deceived and flattered them and led them only too easily to their destruction. If the rest of his life was spent as much over purely tactical problems, as much in consideration of what method it was best for revolutionary leaders to adopt in the interests of their uncomprehending flock, as in the analysis of its actual condition, this was largely due to the lesson of the German revolution. In 1849, after the failure of the risings in Vienna and in Dresden, he wrote violent diatribes against liberals of all persuasions as being cowards and *saboteurs*, still hypnotized by the king and his drill sergeants, frightened by the thought of too definite a victory, prepared to betray the revolution for fear of the dangerous forces which it might release, and so virtually defeated before they began. He declared that, even if the bourgeoisie succeeded in making its corrupt deal with the enemy at the expense of its allies among the *petite bourgeoisie* and the workers, at best it would not gain more than had been won by French liberals under the July monarchy in France, while at worst the bargain would be repudiated by the king and become the prelude to a new monarchist terror. No other journal in Germany dared to go as far in denouncing the government. The uncompromising directness of these analyses, and the audacity of the conclusions which Marx drew from them, fascinated his readers against their will, although unmistakable signs of panic began to show themselves among the shareholders.

By June 1848 the heroic phase of the Paris revolution had spent itself, and the conservative forces began to rally their strength. The socialist and radical members of the Government, Louis Blanc, Albert, Flocon, were forced to resign. The workers rebelled against the right-wing republicans who remained in power, threw up barricades, and after three days' hand-to-hand fighting in the streets, were dispersed and routed by the National Guard and troops which remained loyal to the Government. The June *émeute* may be considered as the first purely socialist rising in Europe, consciously directed against liberals no less than against legitimists. The followers of Blanqui (who was in prison) called upon the people to seize power and establish an armed dictatorship: the spectre of the Communist Manifesto acquired substance at last; for the first time revolutionary socialism revealed itself in that savage and menacing aspect in which it has appeared ever since to its opponents in every land.

Marx reacted at once. Against the frantic protests of the owners of his newspaper, who looked upon all forms of bloodshed and violence with profound horror, he published a long and fiery leading article, taking as his subject the funeral accorded by the State to the soldiers killed during the riots in Paris:

'The fraternity of the two opposing classes (one of which exploits the other) which in February was inscribed in huge letters upon all the façades of Paris, upon all the prisons and all the barracks . . . this fraternity lasted just so long as the interests of the bourgeoisie could fraternize with the interests of the proletariat. Pedants of the old revolutionary tradition of 1793, socialist systematizers who begged the bourgeoisie to grant favours to the people, and were allowed to preach long sermons . . . needed to lull the proletarian lion to sleep, republicans who wanted the whole of the old bourgeois system, minus the crowned figurehead, legitimists who did not wish to doff their livery but merely to change its cut—these had been the people's allies in the February revolution! Yet what the people hated was not Louis Philippe, but the crowned dominion of a class, capital enthroned. Nevertheless, magnanimous as ever, it fancied it had destroyed its own enemies when it had merely overthrown the enemy of its enemies, the common enemy of them all.

'The clashes that spontaneously arise out of the conditions of bourgeois society must be fought to the bitter end; they cannot be conjured out of existence. The best form of State is the one in which opposed social tendencies are not slurred over . . . but secure free expression, and are thus resolved. But we shall be asked: "Have you then no tears, no sighs, no

words of sympathy for the victims of popular frenzy?"
'The State will take due care of the widows and
orphans of these men. They will be honoured in decrees:
they will be given a splendid public funeral: the official
press will proclaim their memories immortal . . . but
the plebeians, tormented by hunger, reviled in the
newspapers, abandoned by even the surgeons, stigma-
tized by all "decent" people as thieves, incendiaries,
convicts, their wives and their children plunged in
greater misery than ever, the best among the survivors
transported—surely the democratic press may claim the
right to crown with laurel their grim and sombre brow?'

This article not unnaturally caused a panic among
the subscribers and the paper began to lose money.
Presently the Prussian Government, by this time convinced it had nothing to fear from popular sentiment,
ordered the dissolution of the democratic assembly. The
latter replied by declaring all taxes imposed by the
government illegal. Marx vehemently supported this
decision and called upon the people to resist attempts to
collect the tax. This time the government acted
promptly and ordered the immediate suppression of the
Neue Rheinische Zeitung. The last issue was printed in
a red type, contained an inflammatory article by Marx
and a magnificent poem by Freiligrath, and was bought
up as a collector's curiosity. Marx was arrested for
incitement to sedition and tried before a Cologne jury.
He turned the occasion into the opportunity of delivering
a speech of great length and erudition in which he
analysed in detail the social and political situation in
Germany and abroad. The result was unexpected: the
foreman of the jury in announcing the acquittal of the
accused said that he wished to thank him in his own

name and that of the jury for an unusually instructive and interesting lecture by which they had all greatly profited. The Prussian Government, which had annulled his Prussian citizenship four years previously, unable to reverse the verdict itself, in July 1849 expelled him from the Rhineland. He went to Paris, where the Bonapartist agitation in favour of the first Napoleon's nephew had made the political situation even more confused than before, and it looked as if something of importance might occur at any moment. His collaborators scattered in various directions: Engels, who disliked inactivity, and declared he had nothing to lose, joined the Paris legion commanded by Willich, a single-minded communist and capable commander, whom Marx detested as a romantic adventurer, and Engels admired for his sincerity, coolness and personal courage. The legion was defeated in Baden by the royal forces without difficulty, and retired in good order to the frontier of the Swiss Confederation, where it dispersed. The majority of the survivors crossed into Switzerland, among them Engels, who preserved the pleasantest memories of his experiences on this occasion, and in later life used to enjoy telling the history of the campaign, which he represented as a gay and agreeable episode of no particular importance. Marx, whose capacity for enjoyment was more limited, found Paris a melancholy place. The revolution had patently failed. Legitimist, Orleanist and Bonapartist intrigue were undermining whatever remained of the democratic structure: such socialists and radicals as had not fled were either in prison or liable to find themselves there at any moment. The appearance of Marx, who was by this time a figure of European notoriety, was highly unwelcome to the government. Soon after his arrival he was presented with the alternative of leaving France or retiring to the distant marshes of the Morbihan in Brittany. Of free countries Belgium was closed to him; Switzerland, which had expelled Weitling and showed little friendliness to Bakunin, was unlikely to permit him to stay: only one European country placed no obstacle in his path. Marx arrived in Paris from the Rhineland in July; a month later a subscription among his friends, among whom Lassalle's name occurs for the first time, enabled him to pay his fare to England. He arrived in London on 24 August 1849; his family followed a month later, and Engels, after dallying in Switzerland, and making a long and agreeable sea voyage from Genoa, came in the beginning of November. He found Marx convinced that the revolution might at any moment break out once more, and engaged on a pamphlet against the conservative French republic.

CHAPTER VIII

EXILE IN LONDON: THE FIRST PHASE

> There is only one antidote to mental suffering, and that is
> physical pain.
>
> KARL MARX, *Herr Vogt.*

MARX arrived in London in 1849 expecting to stay in
England for a few weeks, perhaps months: and in the
event lived there uninterruptedly until his death in 1883.
The isolation of England intellectually and socially
from the main currents of continental life had always
been great, and the middle years of the nineteenth
century offered no exception. The issues which shook
the Continent took many years to cross the English
Channel, and when they did, did so in some new and
peculiar shape, transformed and anglicized in the process of transition. Foreign revolutionaries were on the
whole left unmolested, provided they behaved themselves in an orderly and inconspicuous manner, but
neither was any kind of contact established with them.
Their hosts treated them with correctness and civility,
mingled with a mild indifference to their affairs which
at once irritated and amused them. Revolutionaries
and men of letters, who for many years had spent their
lives in a ferment of intellectual and political activity,
found the London atmosphere inhumanly cold. The
sense of total isolation and exile was brought home
to them even more sharply by the benevolent, distant,
often slightly patronizing manner in which they were
treated by the few Englishmen with whom they came
into contact; and while this tolerant and civilized
attitude did indeed create a vacuum, in which it was

possible to recover physically and morally after the nightmare of 1849, the very distance from events which created this feeling of tranquillity, the immense stability which the capitalist *régime* appeared to possess in England, the complete absence of any symptom of revolution, at times tended to induce a sense of hopeless stagnation which demoralized and embittered all but very few of the men engaged in it. In the case of Marx desperate poverty and squalor were added factors in desiccating his never unduly romantic or pliant character. While these years of enforced inactivity benefited him as a thinker and a revolutionary, they caused him to retire almost entirely into the narrow circle composed of his family, Engels, and a few intimate friends, such as Liebknecht, Wolff and Freiligrath. As a public personality his natural harshness, aggressiveness, and jealousy, his desire to crush all rivals, increased with years; his dislike of the society in which he lived became more and more acute and his personal contact with individual members of it more and more difficult: he quarrelled easily and disliked reconciliation. While he had Engels to lean on he required no other help; and towards the end of his life when the respect and admiration which he received were at their highest, no one else dared to approach him too closely for fear of some particularly humiliating rebuff. Like many great men he liked flattery, and even more, total submission: in his last years he obtained both in full measure, and died in greater honour and material comfort than he had enjoyed during any previous period of his life.

These were the years in which romantic patriots, like Kossuth or Garibaldi, were fêted and publicly cheered in the streets of London; they were regarded as picturesque figures from whom heroic behaviour and noble words were to be expected, rather than as interesting or distinguished men with whom human relations could be established. The majority of their followers were looked upon as harmless eccentrics, as indeed many of them were. Marx, who did not possess sufficient fame or charm to attract such attention, found himself with few friends, and practically penniless, in a country which, although he had visited it less than three years previously, he knew very superficially. He remained in this isolated condition all his life. Living as he did in the midst of an immensely variegated and thriving society, then in the very heyday of the phenomenal growth of its economic and political power, he remained all his life remarkably insulated from it, treating it solely as an object of scientific observation. The collapse of militant radicalism abroad left him no choice, at any rate for a time, but that of a life of observation and scholarship. The important consequence of this was that, since the material upon which he drew was largely English, being confined to what could be found in the library of the British Museum, he relied for the evidence for his hypotheses and generalizations almost entirely on English authors and experience. Those pieces of detailed social and historical research, which form the best and most original chapters in *Das Kapital*, are chiefly occupied with periods for which most of the evidence could be obtained from the financial columns of the *Economist* newspaper, from economic histories, from statistical material to be found in government Blue Books (which he was the first scholar to put to serious scientific use) and other sources to which access could be had without leaving the confines of London.

It was done in the midst of a life spent in ceaseless agitation and practical organizing activity, but with an air of extreme aloofness, as if the writer were situated many miles from the scene of his discussion, a fact which sometimes causes an entirely false impression of Marx, as having grown, during the years of exile, into a remote and detached man of learning who at the age of thirty-two had left the life of action behind him to engage in purely theoretical inquiries.

The moment at which Marx arrived in England was singularly unfavourable to any prospects of the revolution. The mass movement to which continental socialists looked as a model of organized proletarian action among the most highly industrialized and therefore the most socially advanced European nation—Chartism—had lately suffered an overwhelming defeat: foreign observers, including Engels, had seriously over-estimated its strength. It was a loose congeries of heterogeneous interests and persons, and included romantic Tories, advanced radicals influenced by continental models, evangelical reformers, philosophical radicals, dispossessed farmers and artisans, apocalyptic visionaries. They were united by a common horror of the growing pauperization and social degradation of the lower middle class which marked every advance of the industrial revolution; many of them recoiled from all thought of violence and belonged to the class so contemptuously referred to in the Communist Manifesto as 'economists, philanthropists, humanitarian improvers of the conditions of the working class, organizers of charity, members of societies for the prevention of cruelty to animals, temperance fanatics, hole-and-corner reformers of every imaginable kind'.

The movement was badly organized. Its leaders neither agreed among themselves nor possessed individually, and still less collectively, clear beliefs as to the ends to be set before their followers, or the means to be adopted for their realization. The most steadfast members of the movement were those trade unionists of the future, who were principally anxious to improve the conditions and wages of labour, and were interested in wider questions only so far as they concerned their particular cause. It is doubtful whether a serious revolutionary movement could under any circumstances have been created out of this peculiar amalgam. As it was, nothing happened. It may have been the specious relief afforded by the great Reform Bill, or the power of Nonconformity which originally stemmed the tide. At any rate by 1850 the great crisis which had begun in 1847 was over. It was succeeded by the first consciously recognized economic boom in European history, which enormously increased the rate of development of industry and commerce and extinguished the last embers of the Chartist conflagration. Organizers and agitators remained to fight the workers' wrongs, but the exasperated years of Peterloo and the Tolpuddle martyrs, which, in the grim and moving pamphlets of Hodgskin and Bray, and the savage irony of William Cobbett, have left a bitter record of stupid oppression and widespread social ruin, were insensibly giving way to the milder age of John Stuart Mill and the English positivists with their socialist sympathies, the Christian Socialism of the sixties, and the essentially non-political trade-unionism of such prudent and cautious opportunists as Cremer or Lucraft, who distrusted the attempts of foreign doctrinaires to teach them their own business.

Marx naturally began by establishing contact with the German exiles. London at this time contained a conflux of German *émigrés*, members of the dissolved revolutionary committees, exiled poets and intellectuals, vaguely radical German artisans who had settled in England long before the revolution and active communists lately expelled from France or Switzerland, who attempted to reconstitute the Communist League and to renew relations with sympathetic English radicals. Marx followed his usual tactics and kept rigidly to the society of the Germans; he believed firmly that the revolution was not over: indeed he remained convinced of this until the *coup d'état* which placed Louis Napoleon on the throne of France. Meanwhile he spent what he regarded as a mere lull during the battle in the normal activities of political exile, attending meetings of refugees, and quarrelling endlessly with those who incurred his suspicion. The cultured and fastidious Herzen, who was in London at this time, conceived a violent dislike for him, and in his memoirs gave a malicious and brilliant description of the position occupied by Marx and his followers then and later, among the other political *émigrés*. The Germans in general were notoriously incapable of co-operating with the other exiles, Italians, Russians, Poles, Hungarians, whose lack of method and passion for intense personal relations shocked and disgusted them. The latter, for their part, found the Germans equally unattractive; they disliked their woodenness, their coarse manners, their colossal vanity, above all their sordid and unceasing internecine feuds, in the course of which it was usual for intimate details of private life to be dragged into the open and brutally caricatured in the public Press.

The disasters of 1848 did not indeed shake Marx's
theoretical beliefs, but they forced him seriously to
revise his political programme. In the years 1847-8
he was so far influenced by the propaganda of Weitling
and Blanqui as to begin to believe, against his natural,
Hegelian, inclination, that a successful revolution could
be made only by means of a *coup d'état*, carried out by
a small and resolute body of trained revolutionaries, who
having seized power, would hold it, constituting themselves the executive committee of the masses in whose
name they would act. This body would function as
the spear-head of the proletarian attack. The broad
masses of the working class after years of bondage and
darkness cannot be expected to be ripe either for self-
government, or for the control and liquidation of the
forces they have displaced. A party must therefore be
formed which shall function as a political, intellectual,
and legislative *élite* of the people, enjoying its confidence
in virtue of its disinterestedness, its superior training
and its practical insight into the needs of the immediate
situation, able to guide the people's uncertain steps
during the first period of its new freedom. This necessary
interlude he termed the state of permanent revolution,
during which there is the class dictatorship of the
proletariat over the rest 'as a necessary intermediate
step to the abolition of all class distinctions, to the
abolition of all the existing productive relations upon
which these distinctions rest, to the abolition of all social
relations which correspond to these productive relations,
and to the complete reversal of all ideas which derive
from these social relations'. But here, although the end
is clear, the means are left comparatively vague. The
'permanent revolution' is to be brought about by the

dictatorship of the proletariat: but how is this stage to be effected and what form is it to take? There is no doubt that by 1848 Marx thought of it in terms of a self-appointed *élite*: not indeed working in secret, or headed by a single dictatorial figure, as advocated by Bakunin, but as Babeuf had conceived it in 1796, a small body of convinced and ruthless individuals, who were to wield dictatorial power and educate the proletariat until it reached a level at which it comprehended its proper task. It was as a means to this that he advocated in Cologne in 1848-9 a temporary alliance with the leaders of the radical bourgeoisie. The *petite bourgeoisie* struggling against the pressure of the classes immediately above it is the workers' natural ally at this stage: but being unable to rule by its own strength, it will become more and more dependent on the workers' support, until the moment arrives at which the workers, already economic masters of the situation, acquire the official forms of political power, whether by a violent *coup*, or by gradual pressure. This doctrine is familiar to the world because it was adopted by Lenin and was put into practice with the most literal fidelity by him and by Trotsky in Russia in 1917. Marx himself, however, in the light of the events of 1848, abandoned it, at any rate in practice, in vital respects. He discarded the whole conception of the *élite*, which seemed to him powerless to effect anything in the face of a hostile regular army and a supine and untrained proletariat. The leaders of the workers were devoid neither of courage nor of practical sense, yet it would plainly have been quite impossible for them to remain in power in 1848 against the combined force of the royalists, the army and the upper middle class. Unless the proletariat as a whole is made conscious of its historic part, its leaders are helpless. They may provoke an armed rising, but cannot hope to retain its fruits without conscious and intelligent support from the majority of the working class. Consequently, the vital lesson which the events of 1848 contain is, according to Marx, that the first duty of a revolutionary leader is to disseminate among the masses the consciousness of their destiny and their task. Inevitably this is a lengthy and laborious process, but unless it is performed, nothing will be achieved, save the squandering of revolutionary energy in sporadic outbursts led by adventurers and hot-heads, which, having no real basis in the popular will, must inevitably be defeated after a short period of triumph, by the recovered forces of reaction, and be followed by brutal repression which cripples the proletariat for many years to come. On this ground he denounced, on the eve of its occurrence, the revolution which resulted in the Paris Commune of 1871: although later, and largely for tactical motives, he wrote it a moving and eloquent epitaph.

The second point on which he radically changed his views was the possibility of collaboration with the bourgeoisie. Theoretically, he still believed that the dialectic of history necessitated a *petit bourgeois* régime as a prelude to complete communism; but the strength of this class in Germany and France, and its open determination to protect itself against its proletarian ally, convinced him that a compact with it would militate against the workers as the weaker power: the plan to govern from behind the scenes could not be realized yet. This had been the chief point of difference between him and the Cologne communists who had opposed alliance with the liberals as being suicidal opportunism. He now embraced their point of view himself, although not for their reasons: not, that is to say, because opportunism as such was morally degrading or necessarily self-defeating, but because it was in this particular case bound to be unsuccessful, to confuse issues in a party not too securely organized, and so lead to internal weakness and defeat. Hence his continued insistence in later years on preserving the purity of the party, and its freedom from any compromising entanglements. The policy of gradual expansion and the slow conquest of political power through recognized parliamentary institutions, accompanied by systematic pressure on an international scale upon employers through trade unions and similar organizations, as a means of securing improved economic conditions for their workers, which characterizes the tactics of socialist parties in the late nineteenth and early twentieth centuries, was the legitimate product of Marx's analysis of the causes of the catastrophe of the revolutionary year 1848.

His main objective—the creation of conditions in which the dictatorship of the proletariat, 'the permanent revolution', might be realized—was left unaffected: the bourgeoisie and all its institutions were inevitably doomed to extinction. The process might take longer than he had originally supposed; if so, the proletariat must be taught patience; not until the situation itself is ripe for intervention must the leaders call for action: in the meanwhile it must devote itself to husbanding, organizing and disciplining its forces into readiness for the decisive crisis. History has offered a very curious commentary on this conclusion: the makers of the communist revolution in Russia, by acting in accordance with the earlier and discarded view, and striking while the popular masses were palpably unripe for their task, did, at any rate, succeed in averting the consequences of 1848 and 1871 : while the orthodox German and Austrian social democrats, faithful to the master's final doctrine, by moving carefully and with caution, and expending their energy upon the education of the masses to a sense of their mission, were duly overwhelmed by the re-organized reactionary class, whose strength the march of history, and constant sapping on the part of the proletariat, should long before have finally undermined.

Meanwhile no sign of revolution could be detected anywhere, and the mood of irrational optimism was succeeded by one of profound depression. 'One cannot recollect those days without acute pain', wrote Herzen in his memoirs. '. . . France was moving with the velocity of a falling star towards the inevitable *coup d'état*. Germany lay prostrate at the feet of Czar Nicholas, dragged down by wretched, betrayed Hungary. . . . The revolutionaries carried on empty agitation. Even the most serious persons are sometimes overcome by the fascination of mere forms, and manage to convince themselves that they are in fact doing something if they hold meetings with a mass of documents and protocols, conferences at which facts are recorded, decisions are taken, proclamations are printed, and so forth. The bureaucracy of the revolution is capable of losing itself in this sort of thing just as much as real officialdom : England teems with hundreds of associations of this sort : solemn meetings take place which dukes and peers of the realm, clergymen and secretaries, ceremoniously attend : treasurers collect funds, journalists write articles, all are busily engaged in doing nothing at all. These philanthropic or religious gatherings fulfil the double function of serving as a form of amusement and acting as a sop to the troubled consciences of these somewhat worldly Christians. . . . The whole thing was a contradiction in terms: an open conspiracy, a plot concocted behind open doors.'

In the sultry atmosphere of continual intrigue, suspicion and recrimination which fills the early years of any large political emigration whose members are bound to each other by circumstances rather than by any clearly conceived common cause, Marx spent his first two years in London. He resolutely declined to have any dealings with Herzen, Mazzini and their associates, but he was not inactive. He edited the *Neue Rheinische Zeitung* as a review, organized committees to help refugees, published a highly successful denunciation of the methods of the police in the Cologne trials of his associates, tracking down and exposing the gross forgeries and perjury perpetrated by its agents; which, if it did not free his comrades, made trials of the same kind more difficult in the future; carried on a vendetta against Willich within the Communist League, and, believing that an institution which promotes half-truths is more dangerous than total inactivity and is better dead, by remorseless intrigue brought about its dissolution. Having thus successfully torpedoed his own former associates, and feeling nothing but contempt for the rest of the emigration as a collection of ineffective and harmless chatterers, he constituted himself and Engels as an independent centre of propaganda, a personal union round which the broken and scattered remnants of German Communism would gradually be gathered into a force once more. The plan was completely successful.

His most important writings of this period are concerned with the recent events in France: his style, often opaque and obscure when dealing with abstract issues, is luminous when dealing with facts. The essays on the *Class Struggle in France*, and the articles reprinted under the title *The Eighteenth Brumaire of Louis Bonaparte*, are models of penetrating and cruel pamphleteering. The two pamphlets cover much of the same ground and give a brilliant, polemical description of the revolution and the second republic, analysing in detail the relations and interplay of the political, economic and personal factors, in terms of the alignment of classes whose needs they embody. In a series of sharp, epigrammatic sketches the leading representatives of the various parties are classified and assigned to the classes on whose support they depend. The evolution of the political situation from vague liberalism to the conservative republic, and thence to the open class-struggle, ending in naked despotism, is represented as a travesty of the events of 1789: then every successive phase was more violent and revolutionary than the last; in 1848 the exact reverse occurred: in June the proletariat was deserted and betrayed by its *petit bourgeois* allies; later those were in their turn abandoned by the middle class; finally they too were outmanœuvred by the great landowners and financiers and delivered into the hands of the army and Louis Napoleon. Nor could this have been prevented by a different policy on the part of individual politicians since it was the inescapable result of the stage of historical development reached by French society at this time.

Marx's other activities at this period included popular

lectures on political economy to the German Workers'
Educational Union, and finally a considerable correspondence with the German revolutionaries now
scattered everywhere, and notably with Engels, who
reluctantly and unhappily, having no other means of
supporting himself, made his peace with his parents
and settled down in Manchester to work in the office
of his father's firm of cotton-spinners. The comparative
security which he obtained by this means he used to
support Marx, materially and intellectually, during the
remainder of his life. Marx's own financial position
was for many years desperate: he had no regular source
of income, a growing family, and a reputation which
precluded the possibility of employment by any respectable concern. The squalid poverty in which he and his
family lived during the next twenty years, and the
unspeakable humiliations which this entailed, have
often been described: at first the family wandered from
one hovel to another, from Chelsea to Leicester Square
and thence to the disease-ridden slums of Soho; often
there was no money to pay the tradesmen and the family
would literally starve until a loan or the arrival of a
pound note from Engels temporarily eased the situation;
sometimes the entire clothing of the family was in pawn,
and they were forced to sit for hours without light or
food, interrupted only by the visits of dunning creditors,
who were met on the doorstep by one or other of the
children with the unvarying and automatic answer,
'Mr. Marx ain't upstairs.'

A lively description of the conditions in which he
lived during the first seven years of exile survives in
the report of a Prussian spy who somehow contrived
to worm his way into the Dean Street establishment:

'. . . He lives in one of the worst and cheapest neighbourhoods in London. He occupies two rooms. There is not one clean or decent piece of furniture in either room, everything is broken, tattered, and torn, with thick dust over everything . . . manuscripts, books and newspapers lie beside the children's toys, bits and pieces from his wife's sewing basket, cups with broken rims, dirty spoons, knives, forks, lamps, an inkpot, tumblers, pipes, tobacco ash—all piled up on the same table. On entering the room smoke and tobacco fumes make your eyes water to such an extent that at first you seem to be groping about in a cavern—until you get used to it, and manage to make out certain objects in the haze. Sitting down is a dangerous business. Here is a chair with only three legs, there another which happens to be whole, on which the children are playing at cooking. That is the one that is offered to the visitor, but the children's cooking is not removed, and if you sit down you risk a pair of trousers. But all these things do not in the least embarrass Marx or his wife. You are received in the most friendly way and are cordially offered pipes, tobacco, and whatever else there may happen to be. Presently a clever and interesting conversation arises which repays for all the domestic deficiencies and this makes the discomfort bearable . . .'[1]

A man of genius forced to live in a garret, to go into hiding when his creditors grow importunate, or to lie in bed because his clothes are pawned, is a conventional subject of gay and sentimental comedy. Marx was not a bohemian, and his misfortunes affected him tragically.

[1] Quoted from *Karl Marx, Man and Fighter*, by B. Nicolaievsky and O. Maenchen-Helfen.

He was proud, excessively thin-skinned, and made great demands upon the world: the petty humiliations and insults to which his condition exposed him, the frustration of his desire for the commanding position to which he thought himself entitled, the repression of his colossal natural vitality, made him turn in upon himself in paroxysms of hatred and of rage. His bitter feeling often found outlet in his writings and in long and savage personal vendettas. He saw plots, persecution, and conspiracies everywhere; the more his victims protested their innocence, the more convinced he became of their duplicity and their guilt.

His mode of living consisted of daily visits to the British Museum reading-room, where he normally remained from nine in the morning until it closed at seven; this was followed by long hours of work at night, accompanied by ceaseless smoking, which from a luxury had become an indispensable anodyne; this affected his health permanently and he became liable to frequent attacks of a disease of the liver sometimes accompanied by boils and an inflammation of the eyes, which interfered with his work, exhausted and irritated him, and interrupted his never certain means of livelihood. 'I am plagued like Job, though not so God-fearing', he wrote in 1858. 'Everything that these gentlemen [the doctors] say boils down to the fact that one ought to be a prosperous *rentier* and not a poor devil like me, as poor as a church mouse.' Engels, whose annual income during those years does not appear to have exceeded one hundred pounds, with which, as his father's representative, he had to keep up a respectable establishment in Manchester, could not, with all his generosity, afford much systematic help at first: occasionally, friends in

Cologne, or generous German socialists like Liebknecht or Freiligrath, managed to collect small sums for him, which, together with fees for occasional journalism, and occasional small legacies from relatives, enabled him to continue on the very brink of subsistence. It is not therefore difficult to understand that he hated poverty, and the vicious slavery and degradation which it entails, more passionately even than servility. The descriptions scattered in his works of life in industrial slums, in mining villages or plantations, and of the attitude of civilized opinion towards them, are given with a combination of violent indignation and frigid, wholly unhysterical bitterness, which, particularly when his account grows detailed and his tone grows unnaturally quiet and flat, possess a frightening quality and induce intolerable anger and shame in readers left unmoved by the fiery rhetoric of Carlyle, by the dignified and humane pleading of J. S. Mill, or by the sweeping eloquence of William Morris and the Christian Socialists. During these years three of his children, his two sons Guido and Edgar, and his daughter Franziska died, largely as a result of the conditions in which they lived. When Franziska died he had no money to pay for a coffin, and was rescued only by the generosity of a French refugee. The incident is described in harrowing detail in a letter written by Frau Marx to a fellow exile. She was herself often ill, and the children were looked after by their devoted family servant, Helene Demuth, who remained with them until the end.

'I could not and cannot fetch the doctor', he wrote to Engels on one of these occasions, 'because I have no money for the medicine. For the last eight or ten days I have fed my family on bread and potatoes, and to-day it is still doubtful whether I shall be able to obtain even these.'

He was uncommunicative by nature, and less than anyone who has ever lived given to self-pity; indeed, in his letters to Engels he sometimes satirized his own misfortunes with a grim irony which may conceal from the casual reader the desperate condition in which he frequently found himself. But when in 1856, his son Edgar, of whom he was very fond, died at the age of six, it broke through even his iron reserve: 'I have suffered every kind of misfortune', he wrote to his friend, 'but I have only just learnt what real unhappiness is . . . in the midst of all the suffering which I have gone through in these days the thought of you, and your friendship, and the hope that we may still have something reasonable to do in this world, has kept me upright. . . .

'Bacon says that really important people have so many contacts with nature and the world, have so much to interest them, that they easily get over any loss. I am not of those important people. My child's death has affected me so greatly that I feel the loss as bitterly as on the first day. My wife is also completely broken down.'

The only form of pleasure which the family could allow itself was an occasional picnic on Hampstead Heath during the summer months. They used to set out on Sunday morning from the house in Dean Street, and, accompanied by the faithful Lenchen Demuth and one or two friends, carrying a basket of food and newspapers bought on the way, walked to Hampstead. There they would sit under the trees, and while the children played or picked flowers, their elders would talk or read or sleep. As the afternoon wore on, the mood grew gayer and gayer, particularly when the jovial Engels was present. They made jokes, sang, ran races, Marx recited poetry, which he was fond of doing, took the children for rides on his back, entertained everyone, and, as a final turn, would solemnly mount and ride a donkey up and down in front of the party: a sight which never failed to give general pleasure. At nightfall they would walk back, often singing patriotic German or English songs on their way home to Soho. These agreeable occasions were, however, few and rare, and did little to lighten what Marx himself in one of his letters to Engels called the sleepless night of exile.

To this condition some slight relief was brought by the sudden invitation to write regular articles on affairs in Europe for the *New York Daily Tribune*. The offer was made by Charles Augustus Dana, its foreign editor, who had been introduced to Marx by Freiligrath in Cologne in 1849, and was greatly impressed by his political shrewdness. The *New York Tribune* was a radical newspaper, founded by a group of American followers of Fourier, which had at this period a circulation of over 200,000 copies, then probably the greatest of any newspaper in the world; its outlook was broadly progressive: in internal affairs it pursued an anti-slavery, free trade policy, while in foreign affairs it attacked the principle of autocracy, and so found itself in opposition to virtually every government in Europe. Marx, who stubbornly refused offers of collaboration with Continental journals the tendency of which he thought reactionary, accepted this offer with alacrity. The new correspondent was to be paid one pound sterling per article. For nearly ten years he wrote weekly dispatches for it roaming over a wide field of subjects, which are of some interest even now. Dana's first request to him was to write a series of articles on the strategy and tactics of both armies during the civil war in Germany and Austria, together with general comments on the art of modern warfare. As Marx was entirely ignorant of the latter subject and had at this period very little English, he found the request far from easy to fulfil: but to refuse anything which offered a steady if meagre source of income was unthinkable. In his perplexity he turned to Engels, who, as on so many occasions in later life, readily and obligingly wrote the articles and signed them with Marx's name. Henceforward, whenever the subject was unknown or uncongenial to him, or he was prevented from working by absence or ill-health, Engels was called upon, and performed his task with such efficiency that the *Tribune's* London correspondent soon acquired a considerable popularity in America as an exceptionally versatile and well-informed journalist, with a definite public of his own.

Engels's articles on the German revolution were re-printed as a pamphlet by Marx called *The German Revolution and Counter Revolution*, and end with the assurance that the revolution is about to break out with even greater violence in the near future. Later the friends admitted they were over-optimistic. Marx formulated the celebrated generalization that only an economic slump can lead to a successful revolution; thus the revolution of 1848 was nurtured in the economic collapse of 1847, and the boom of 1851 removed all hope of imminent political conflagration.

Henceforth the attention of both is concentrated upon detecting symptoms of a major economic crisis. Engels from his office in Manchester filled his letters

with information about the state of world markets;
gold losses by the Bank of England, the bankruptcy
of a Hamburg bank, a bad harvest in France or America,
are noted exultantly as indicating that the great crisis
cannot be far off. In 1857 a genuine slump did at last
occur on the required scale. It was not, however, except
in agricultural Italy, followed by any revolutionary
developments. After this there is less mention of inevitable crises, and more discussion of the organization of
a revolutionary party. The acute disappointment had
left its effect.

While Engels dealt with the military intelligence
required by the American public, Marx published a
rapid succession of articles on English politics, internal
and external, on foreign policy, on Chartism, and the
character of the various English ministries, which he
became expert at summing up in a few malicious
sentences, usually at the expense of *The Times*, which
always remained his bugbear. He wrote a good deal
about the English rule in India and in Ireland. India
was, he declared, bound in any case to have been conquered by a stronger power:

'The question is not whether the English had any
right to conquer India, but whether we should have
preferred her to have been conquered by Turks or
Persians, or Russians. . . . Of course it is impossible
to compel the English bourgeoisie to want the emancipation or improvement of the social condition of the
Indian masses, which depends not only on the development of the forces of production, but on the ownership
of them by the people. But what it can do is to create
the material conditions for the realization of this double
need.'

And again: 'However melancholy we may find', he wrote in 1853, 'the spectacle of the ruin and desolation of these tens of thousands of industrious, peaceful, patriarchal, social groups . . . suddenly cut off from their ancient civilization and their traditional means of existence, we must not forget that these idyllic village communities . . . always provided a firm basis to oriental despotism, confining the human intelligence within the narrowest limits, making of it the obedient traditional instrument of superstition, stunting its growth, robbing it . . . of all capacity of historical activity; let us not forget the egoism of barbarians who, concentrated on an insignificant portion of earth's surface, watched unmoved while immense empires crumbled, unspeakable cruelties were committed, the populations of entire cities were butchered—observed this as if they were events in nature, and so themselves became the helpless victims of every invader who happened to turn his attention to them. . . . In causing social revolution in India, England was, it is true, guided by the lowest motives, and conducted it dully and woodenly. But that is not the point. The question is whether humanity can fulfil its purpose without a complete social revolution in Asia. If not, then England, in spite of all her crimes, was the unconscious instrument of history in bringing about this revolution.'

Of Ireland he said that the cause of English labour was inextricably bound up with the liberation of Ireland, whose cheap labour was a continual threat to the English unions; her economic subjection, as in the analogous cases of serfdom in Russia and slavery in the United States, must be abolished before Ireland's English masters, among whom the English working class (who treated the Irish much as the 'poor whites' of the Southern states of America treated the negroes) must be included, could hope to emancipate themselves and create a free society. In both cases he consistently underestimated the force of rising nationalism: his hatred of all separatism, as of all institutions founded on some purely traditional or emotional basis, blinded him to their actual influence. In a similar spirit Engels, writing of the Czechs, observed that the nationalism of the Western Slavs was an artificially preserved, unreal phenomenon, which could not long resist the advance of the superior German culture. Such absorption was a fate inevitably in store for all small and local civilizations, in virtue of the force of historical gravitation which causes the smaller to be merged in the greater: a tendency which all progressive parties should actively encourage. Both Marx and Engels believed that nationalism, together with religion and militarism, were so many anachronisms, at once the by-products and the bulwarks of the capitalist order, irrational, counter-revolutionary forces which, with the passing of their material foundation, would automatically disappear. Marx's own tactical policy with regard to them was to consider whether in a given case they operated for or against the proletarian cause, and to decide in accordance with this criterion alone, whether they were to be supported or attacked. Thus he favoured it in India and in Ireland, because it was a weapon in the fight against imperialism, and attacked the democratic nationalism of Mazzini or Kossuth because in such countries as Italy, Hungary or Poland, it seemed to him to work merely for the replacement of a foreign by a native system of capitalist exploitation, and so to obstruct the social revolution. Among English politicians he attacked Russell as a pseudo-radical who betrayed his cause at every step, but his *bête noire* was undoubtedly Palmerston, whom he accused of being a disguised Russophile, and mocked for his sentimental support of small nationalities in Europe. He was, however, a connoisseur of political skill in all its forms, and confessed to a certain admiration of the *élan* and adroitness with which that cynical and light-hearted statesman carried off his most unscrupulous strokes.

His attacks on Palmerston brought him into contact with an exceedingly odd and remarkable figure. David Urquhart had in his youth been in the Diplomatic Service, and after becoming a warm Philhellene in Athens had been transferred to Constantinople, where he conceived a violent and life-long passion for Islam and the Turks, the 'purity' of whose constitution he admired, and for the Church of Rome, with which he remained on excellent terms, although he was born and died a Calvinist; with this he combined an equally violent hatred for Whigs, free trade, the Church of England, industrialism, and, in particular, the Russian Empire, whose malevolent and omnipotent influence he regarded as responsible for all the evils in Europe. This eccentric figure, a picturesque survival from a more spacious age, sat in Parliament as an Independent for many years, and published a newspaper and numerous tracts devoted almost entirely to the single purpose of exposing Palmerston, whom he accused of being a hired agent of the Czar, engaged in a life-long attempt to subvert the moral order of Western Europe in his master's interest. Even Palmerston's attitude during the Crimean War did not shake him: he explained it as a cunning ruse to cloak the nature of his real activities; hence his deliberate sabotage of the entire campaign, which was clearly designed to do Russia as little damage as possible. Marx, who had somehow arrived at the same curious conclusion, was no less genuinely convinced of Palmerston's venality. The two men met and formed an alliance; Urquhart published anti-Palmerstonian pamphlets by Marx while Marx became an official Urquhartite, contributed to Urquhart's paper and appeared on the platforms of his meetings. His articles were later published as pamphlets. The most peculiar are *Palmerston, What Has He Done?* and *The Secret Diplomatic History of the Eighteenth Century*, both of which were devoted to exposing the hidden hand of Russia in all major European disasters. Each was under the impression that he was skilfully using the other for his own ends: Marx thought Urquhart a harmless monomaniac of whom use might be made; Urquhart, for his part, thought highly of Marx's abilities as a propagandist, and on one occasion congratulated him on possessing an intelligence worthy of a Turk. This bizarre association continued harmoniously, if intermittently, for a number of years. After the deaths of Palmerston and Czar Nicholas, the alliance was gradually dissolved. Marx obtained a good deal of amusement, and as much financial help as he could extract, from his relationship with his strange patron, of whom he soon grew quite fond; indeed, the latter was unique among his political allies in that their relation continued to be entirely friendly until Urquhart's death.

Marx found few sympathizers among the trade union leaders. The ablest of them either held views not very dissimilar to those of Owen, who by the shining example

of his own achievements, sought to prove the wicked base-
lessness of the doctrine of class war: or else were busy
local labour leaders working for the immediate needs of
this or that trade or industry, dead to wider issues, prepared to welcome all radicals equally in a federation
called 'The Fraternal Democrats', the very name of
which revolted Marx. The only Englishman who stood
at all close to him in those days was Ernest Jones, a revolutionary Chartist, who made a vain attempt to revive
that dying movement. Jones was born and brought up in
Germany and resembled more closely than anyone else
in England the type of continental socialist familiar to
Marx; his views were, especially in later years, too
similar to those of the 'True Socialists' Hess and Grün to
please Marx entirely, but he needed allies, the choice
was limited, and he accepted Jones as the best and
most advanced that England had to offer. Jones, who
conceived a great admiration and affection for Marx and
his household, supplied him with a great deal of information about English conditions; it was he who turned
Marx's attention to the land enclosures which still went
on in Scotland where many hundreds of small tenants
and crofters had been evicted to make room for deer
parks and pasture. The result was a vitriolic article by
Marx in the *New York Tribune* on the private affairs of
the Duchess of Sutherland, who had expressed sympathy
for the cause of the Negro slaves in America. The
article, which is a sketch for the longer passage in *Kapital*,
is a masterpiece of bitter and vehement eloquence,
directly descended from the masterpieces of Voltaire
and Marat, and a model for many later pieces of socialist
invective. The attack is not so much personal as directed
at the system under which a capricious old woman no

more deranged, heartless, and vindictive than the majority of her immediate society, has it in her absolute power, with the full approval of her class and of public opinion, to humiliate, uproot and ruin an entire population of honest and industrious men and women, rendered destitute overnight in a land which was rightfully theirs, since all that was man-made in it they and their ancestors had created by their labour.

Such pieces of social analysis and polemic pleased the American public no less than Marx's dry and ironical articles on foreign affairs. The articles were well-informed, shrewd and detached in tone: they showed no particular power of prescience, nor was there any attempt to give a comprehensive survey of contemporary affairs as a whole: as a commentary on events they were less candid and less interesting than the letters which their author wrote to Engels at this period, but as journalism they were in advance of their time. Marx's method was to present his readers with a brief sketch of events or characters, emphasizing hidden interests and the sinister activity likely to result from them, rather than the explicit motives furnished by the actors themselves, or the social value of this or that measure or policy. This gives his journalism a highly twentieth-century flavour, and exhibits more vividly than his theoretical writings, the genuine difference between his naturalistic, acid, distrustful, ethically neutral attitude, and that of the great majority of the more or less humanitarian and idealistic social historians and critics of his time. At the same time he was engaged in gathering material for the economic treatise which should serve as a weapon against the vague idealism of the loosely connected radical groups, which, in his view, led to confusion both of thought and of action, and paralysed the efforts of such few clear-headed leaders as the workers possessed. He applied himself to the task of establishing, in the place of this, a rigorous doctrine, unambiguous in theory and definite in practice, adherence to which would become at once the test, the reason and the guarantee of a united, and, above all, active body of social revolutionaries. Their strength would derive from their unity, and their unity from the coherence of the practical beliefs which they had in common.

The foundations of his doctrine were embodied in his previous writings, notably in the *Communist Manifesto*. In a letter written in 1852 he carefully stated what he regarded as original in it: 'What I did that was new was to prove (1) that the *existence of classes* is only bound up with particular, historic phases in the development of production; (2) that the class struggle necessarily leads to the *dictatorship of the proletariat*; (3) that this dictatorship itself only constitutes the transition to the *abolition of all classes* and to a classless society.' On these foundations the new movement was to be built.

In a sense he succeeded more rapidly than he could have hoped: the rise and swift growth upon the ruins of 1848 of a new and militant party of socialist workers in Germany created for him a sphere of new practical activity in which the latter half of his life was spent. This party was not indeed created by him, but his ideas, and above all a belief in the political programme which he had elaborated, inspired its leaders. He was consulted and approached at every turn; everyone knew that he, and he alone, had inspired the movement and created its basis; to him all questions of theory and practice were instinctively referred; he was admired, feared, suspected and obeyed. Yet the German workers did not look to him as their foremost representative and champion: the man who had organized them into a party and ruled it with absolute power was Marx's junior by several years, born and brought up under similar conditions, but in temper and in outlook more unlike and even opposed to him than at the time either explicitly admitted.

Ferdinand Lassalle, who created German Social Democracy and led it during its first heroic years, was one of the most ardent public personalities of the nineteenth century. By birth a Silesian Jew, by profession a lawyer, by temperament a romantic revolutionary, he was a man whose outstanding characteristics were his intelligence, his vanity, his boundless energy and self-confidence. Since most of the normal avenues of advancement were barred to him on account of his race and his religion, he threw himself with immense passion into the revolutionary movement, where his exceptional ability, his enthusiasm, but most of all his genius as an agitator and a popular orator swiftly raised him to leadership. During the German revolution he delivered inflammatory speeches against the Government, for which he was tried and imprisoned. During the years which followed the period of recantations and dishonour, when Marx and Engels were in exile, and Liebknecht alone among the original leaders who remained in Germany remained faithful to the cause of socialism, Lassalle took upon himself the task of creating a new and better organized proletarian party upon the ruins of 1848. He conceived himself in the part of its sole leader and inspirer, its intellectual, moral and political dictator. He accomplished this task with brilliant success. His beliefs were derived in equal parts from Hegel and from Marx: from the latter he derived the doctrines of economic determinism, of the class struggle, of the inevitability of exploitation in capitalist society. But he rejected the condemnation of the state in the name of society, refusing to follow Proudhon and Marx in regarding the former as a mere coercive instrument of the ruling class, and accepting the Hegelian thesis, according to which the state, even in its present condition, constitutes the highest function of a collection of human beings assembled to lead a common life. He strongly believed in centralization and, up to a point, in internal national unity: in later years he began to believe in the possibility of an anti-bourgeois coalition between the king, the aristocracy, the army, and the workers, culminating in an authoritarian collectivist state, headed by the monarch, and organized in the interests of the only truly productive, i.e. the labouring, class.

His relations with Marx and Engels had never been wholly easy: he declared that Marx was in theoretical matters his master, and treated him with nervous respect. He heralded him everywhere as a man of genius, arranged for the German publication of his books, and otherwise strove to be of service to him in many ways. Marx grudgingly recognized the value of Lasalle's energy, and his organizing ability, but was repelled by him personally, and was deeply suspicious of him politically. He disliked his ostentation, his extravagance, his vanity, his histrionic manners, his loud public profession of his tastes, his opinions and his ambitions; he detested the very brilliance of his impressionistic surveys of social and political facts, which seemed to him flimsy, superficial, and fallacious by comparison with his own painful and laborious thoroughness: he disliked and distrusted the temperamental and capricious control which Lassalle exercised over the workers, and, even more, his absorbed flirtation with the enemy. Finally, he felt jealous and possessive about a movement which owed to him both its practical policy and its intellectual foundations, and now seemed to have deserted him, infatuated by a political *femme fatale*, a specious, glittering adventurer, an avowed opportunist both in private life and in public policy, guided by no fixed plan, attached to no principle, moving towards no clear goal. Nevertheless, a certain intimacy of relations existed between them, or if not intimacy, a mutual appreciation. Lassalle was born and brought up under intellectual influences similar to his own, they fought against the same enemy, and on all fundamental issues spoke the same language, which Proudhon, Bakunin, and the English trade unionists had never done, and the former young Hegelians had long ceased to do. Moreover, he was a man of action, a genuine revolutionary, and absolutely fearless. Each recognized that with, perhaps, the exception of Engels, the other possessed a higher degree of political intelligence, penetration, and practical courage than any other member of their party. They understood each other instinctively, and found communication both easy and exhilarating: when Marx went to Berlin, he stayed quite naturally with Lassalle. When Lassalle came to London, he stayed with Marx, and maddened his proud and sensitive host, then in the last stage of penury, by the mere fact of being a witness of his condition, and even more by his gay patter and easy extravagance, spending more on cigars and buttonholes

than Marx and his family spent on a week's livelihood. There was some difficulty, too, about a sum of
money which Marx had borrowed from him. Of all this
Lassalle, it seems, was totally unaware, being exceptionally insensitive to his surroundings, as vigorous and
flamboyant natures often are. Marx never forgot his
humiliation, and after Lassalle's London visit their
relations deteriorated abruptly.

Lassalle created the new party by a method still novel
in his day, and employed only sporadically by the
English Chartists, although familiar enough later: he
undertook a series of highly publicized political tours
through the industrial areas of Germany, making fiery
and seditious speeches which overwhelmed his proletarian audiences and roused them to immense enthusiasm. There and then he formed them into sections of
the new workers' movement, organized as an official,
legally constituted party, thus breaking openly with the
old method of small revolutionary cells which met in
secret and carried on underground propaganda. His
last journey among his followers was a triumphal tour
over conquered territory: it strengthened his already
unique influence upon German workers of all types, ages
and professions.

The theoretical foundations of the programme were
borrowed, largely from Marx, and perhaps to some
extent from the radical Prussian economist Rodbertus-
Jagetzow, but the party had many strongly non-Marxist
characteristics: it was not specifically organized for a
revolution; it was opportunist, and prepared for alliance
with other anti-bourgeois parties; it was nationalistic
and largely confined to German conditions and needs,
One of its foremost ends was the development of a

workers' co-operative system, not indeed as an alternative to, but as an intrinsic element in, political action,
to be organized or financed by the state, yet still sufficiently similar to Proudhon's anti-political mutualism,
and the politically sluggish English trade unionism, to
incur open hostility from Marx. Moreover, it had been
created by means of the personal ascendancy of one
individual. There was a strong emotional element in
the unquestioned dictatorship which Lassalle exercised
in his last years, a form of hero-worship which Marx,
who disliked every form of unreason, and distrusted
spell-binders in politics, instinctively abhorred. Lassalle
introduced into German socialism the theory that
circumstances might occur in which something like a
genuine alliance might be formed with the absolutist
Prussian government against the industrial bourgeoisie.
This was the kind of opportunism which Marx must
have considered the most ruinous of all possible defects;
the experience of 1848, if it taught no other lesson, had
conclusively demonstrated the fatal consequence to a
young, and as yet comparatively defenceless, party of
an alliance with a well-established older party, fundamentally hostile to its demands, in which each attempts
to exploit the other, and the better armed force inevitably
wins. Marx, as was made evident from his address to
the Central Communist Committee in 1850, considered
himself to have erred seriously in supposing that an
alliance with the radical bourgeoisie was possible and
even necessary before the final victory of the proletariat.
But even he had never dreamed of an alliance with the
feudal nobility for the purpose of delivering an attack
on individualism as such, merely for the sake of attaining
some kind of state control. Such a move he regarded as

a typical Bakuninist caricature of his own policy and aspirations.

Both Marx and Engels were fundamentally solid German democrats in their attitude to the masses, and instinctively reacted against the seeds of romantic fascism which can now be so clearly discerned in Lassalle's beliefs and acts and speeches, particularly in his passionate patriotism, his romantic version of himself as the dedicated leader, his belief in a state-planned economy controlled, at any rate for a time, by the military aristocracy, his advocacy of armed intervention by Germany on the side of the French Emperor in the Italian campaign (which he defended against Marx and Engels on the ground that only a war would precipitate a German revolution), his unconcealed sympathy with Mazzini and the Polish nationalists, finally his belief, on which the National Socialism of our day offers a curious commentary, that the existing machinery of the Prussian state can be used to aid the *petite bourgeoisie* as well as the proletariat of Germany against the growing encroachment of merchants, industrialists and bankers. He actually went to the length of negotiating with Bismarck on these lines, each being under the impression that, when the time came, he could use the other as a cat's-paw for his own ends: each recognized and admired the other's audacity, intelligence, and freedom from petty scruple; they vied with each other in the candour of their political realism, in their open contempt for their mediocre followers, and in their admiration for power and success as such. Bismarck liked vivid personalities, and in later years used to refer to these conversations with pleasure, saying that he never hoped to meet so interesting a man again. How

far Lassalle had in fact gone in this direction was
subsequently revealed by the discovery in 1928 of
Bismarck's private record of the negotiations. They
were cut short by Lassalle's early death in a duel, which
arose out of a casual love-affair. If he had lived, and
Bismarck had chosen to continue to play on his almost
megalomaniac vanity, Lassalle would in the end almost
certainly have lost, and the newly created party might
have foundered long before it did; indeed, as a theorist
of state supremacy and as a demagogue, Lassalle should
be counted among the founders not only of European
socialism, but equally of the doctrine of personal
dictatorship and fascism, which doubtless is precisely
what had attracted Bismarck.

In the subsequent conflict between the Marxists and
the Lassalleans, Marx won a formal victory which saved
the purity of his own doctrine and political method, not,
oddly enough, for Germany, for which it was primarily
intended, but for application in far more primitive
countries which scarcely entered his thoughts, Russia,
China, and, up to a point, Spain and Mexico. The
report of Lassalle's death in the spring of 1864 roused
little sympathy in either Marx or Engels. To both it
seemed a typically foolish end to a career of absurd
self-dramatization. Lassalle, had he lived, might well
have proved an obstacle of the first magnitude. Yet the
relief, at least in the case of Marx, was not unmixed with
a certain sentimental regret for the passing of so familiar
a figure on whom he looked, in spite of all his failings,
with something not wholly unlike affection. Lassalle
was a German and a Hegelian, inextricably connected
with the events of 1848, and his own revolutionary past:
a man who, in spite of all his colossal defects, stood head

and shoulders above the pygmies among whom he moved, creatures into whom he had for a brief hour infused his own vitality, and who would soon sink exhausted into their old apathy, appearing even smaller, pettier, meaner than before.

'He was, after all, one of the old stock,' he wrote, 'the enemy of our enemies . . . it is difficult to believe that so noisy, stirring, pushing a man is now as dead as a mouse, and must hold his tongue altogether . . . the devil knows, the crowd is getting smaller and no new blood is coming forward.'

The news of Lassalle's death sent him into one of his rare moods of personal melancholy, almost of despair, very different from the cloud of anger and resentment in which he normally lived. He suddenly became over-whelmed by the sense of his own total isolation, and the hopelessness of all individual endeavour in the face of the triumphant European reaction, a feeling which the tranquillity and monotony of life in England sooner or later induced in all the exiled revolutionaries. Indeed the very respect, and even admiration with which many of them spoke of English life and English institutions, were an implicit acknowledgement of their own personal failure, their loss of faith in the power of mankind to achieve its own emancipation. They saw themselves gradually sinking into a cautious, almost cynical, quietism which they themselves knew to be an admission of defeat and a complete stultification of a life spent in warfare, the final collapse of the ideal world in which they had invested beyond recovery everything that they themselves possessed, and much that belonged to others. This mood, with which Herzen, Mazzini, Kossuth were intimately acquainted, was with Marx uncommon: he was genuinely convinced that the process of history was both inevitable and progressive, and this intense belief excluded all possibility of doubt or disillusionment on fundamental issues; he had never relied on reason or the idealism of individuals or of the masses as decisive factors in social evolution, and having staked nothing, lost nothing in the great intellectual and moral bankruptcy of the 'sixties and 'seventies. All his life he strove to destroy or diminish the influence of popular leaders and demagogues who believed in the power of the individual to alter the destinies of nations. His savage attacks on Proudhon and Lassalle, his later duel with Bakunin, were not mere moves in the struggle for personal supremacy on the part of an ambitious and despotic man resolved to destroy all possible rivals. It is true that he was by nature almost insanely jealous: nevertheless, mingled with his personal feelings there was genuine indignation with the gross errors of judgement of which these men seemed to him too often guilty: and, even more strongly felt, ironical as it may seem when his own position is remembered, a violent disapproval of the influence of dominant individuals as such, of the element of personal power, which, by creating a false relation between the leader and his followers, is, sooner or later, bound to blind both to the demands of the objective situation.

Yet it remains the case that the unique position of authority which he himself occupied in international socialism during the last decade of his life, did far more to consolidate and ensure the adoption of his system than mere attention to his works or the consideration of history in the light of them could ever have achieved. His writings during these years make depressing reading:

apart from journalism in German and American papers, and literary hackwork forced on him by his poverty, he confined himself almost entirely to polemical tracts, the longest of which, *Herr Vogt*, written in 1860, was designed to clear his own name from the imputation of having brought his friends into unnecessary danger during the Cologne trials, and to counter-attack his accuser, a well-known Swiss naturalist and radical politician, Karl Vogt, by alleging that he was in the pay of the French Emperor. It is of interest only for the melancholy light which it throws on ten years of frustration, filled with squabbles and intrigues, which succeeded the heroic age. In 1859 he finally published his *Critique of Political Economy*, but it was little read: its main theses were much more impressively stated eight years later, in the first volume of *Das Kapital*.

His faith in the ultimate victory of his cause remained unaffected even during the darkest years of the reaction. Speaking in the early 'fifties at a dinner given to the compositors and staff of *The People's Paper*, in answer to the toast 'The proletarians of Europe' he declared: 'In our days everything seems pregnant with its contradiction. Machinery gifted with the wonderful power of shortening and fructifying human labour we behold starving and overworking it. The victories of art seem bought by the loss of character. Even the pure light of science seems able to shine only against the dark background of ignorance. . . . This antagonism between modern industry and science on the one hand, and modern misery and dissolution on the other, this antagonism between the productive forces and the social relations of our epoch is a fact, palpable and overwhelming. Some may bewail it, others may wish to get rid of modern arts in order to get rid of modern conflicts. . . . For our part we do not mistake the shape of the shrewd spirit that continues to mark these contradictions . . . we recognize our old friend, Robin Goodfellow, the old mole that can work in the earth so fast . . . the Revolution.' It must have seemed a singularly unplausible thesis to the majority of his listeners: certainly the events of the years which followed did little to bear out his prophecy.

In 1860 Marx's fame and influence were confined to a narrow circle: interest in communism had died down since the Cologne trials in 1851; with the phenomenal development of industry and commerce, faith in liberalism, in science, in peaceful progress, began to mount once more. Marx himself was almost beginning to acquire the interest of a historical figure, to be regarded as the formidable theorist and agitator of a former generation, now exiled and destitute, and supporting himself by casual journalism in an obscure corner of London. Fifteen years later all this had altered. Still comparatively unknown in England, he had grown abroad into a figure of vast fame and notoriety, regarded by some as the instigator of every revolutionary movement in Europe, the fanatical dictator of a world movement pledged to subvert the moral order, the peace, happiness and prosperity of mankind. By these he was represented as the evil genius of the working class, plotting to sap and destroy the peace and morality of civilized society, systematically exploiting the worst passions of the mob, creating grievances where none existed, pouring vinegar in the malcontents' wounds, exacerbating their relations with their employers in order to create the universal chaos in which everyone would lose, and so finally all would be made level at last, the rich and the poor, the bad and the good, the industrious and the idle, the just and the unjust. Others saw in him the most indefatigable and devoted strategist and tactician of labouring classes everywhere, the infallible authority on all theoretical questions, the creator of an irresistible movement designed to over-throw the prevailing rule of injustice and inequality by persuasion or by violence. To them he appeared as an angry and indomitable modern Moses, the leader and saviour of all the insulted and the oppressed, with the milder and more conventional Engels at his side, an Aaron ready to expound his words to the benighted, half-comprehending masses of the proletariat. The event which more than any other was responsible for this transformation was the creation of the first Workers' International in 1864, which radically altered the character and history of European socialism.

CHAPTER IX

THE INTERNATIONAL

The French Revolution is the precursor of another, more magnificent revolution which will be the last.

GRACCHUS BABEUF, *Manifeste des Egaux*, 1796

THE First International came into being in the most casual possible fashion. In spite of the efforts of various organizations and committees to co-ordinate the activities of the workers of various countries, no genuine ties between them had been established. This was due to several causes. Since the general character of such bodies was conspiratorial, only a small minority of radically minded, fearless and 'advanced' workers were attracted to them; moreover, it was generally the case that before anything concrete could be achieved, a foreign war, or repressive measures by governments, put an end to the existence of the secret committees. To this must be added the lack of acquaintance and sympathy between the workers of different nations, working under totally different conditions. And finally, the increased economic prosperity which succeeded the years of hunger and revolt, by raising the general standard of living, automatically made for greater individualism, and stimulated the personal ambition of the bolder and more politically minded workers towards local self-improvement and the pursuit of immediate ends, and away from the comparatively nebulous ideal of an international alliance against the bourgeoisie. The development of the German workers, led by Lassalle, is a typical example of such a purely internal movement, rigorously centralized but confined to a single land, spurred on by an optimistic hope of gradually forcing the capitalist enemy to terms by the sheer weight of numbers, without having recourse to a revolutionary upheaval or violent seizure of power. This was encouraged by Bismarck's anti-bourgeois policy which appeared to weight the scales in favour of the workers. In France the fearful defeat of 1848-9 left the city proletariat broken, and for many years incapable of action on a large scale, healing its wounds by forming small local associations more or less Proudhonist in inspiration. Nor were they entirely discouraged in this by the government of Napoleon III. The Emperor himself had in his youth posed as a friend of the peasants, artisans and factory workers against capitalist bureaucracy, and wished to represent his monarchy as an entirely novel and infinitely subtle form of government, an original blend of monarchism, republicanism and Tory democracy, a kind of New Deal in which political absolutism was tempered by economic liberalism; while the government, although centralized and responsible to the Emperor alone, in theory rested ultimately on the confidence of the people, and was therefore to be an entirely new and thoroughly modern institution, infinitely sensitive to new needs, responsive to every nuance of social change.

Part of Napoleon's elaborate policy of social conciliation was the preservation of a delicate balance of power between the classes by playing them off against each other. The workers were therefore permitted to form themselves into unions under strict police supervision, in order to offset the dangerously growing power of the financial aristocracy with its suspected Orleanist loyalties. The workers, with no alternative choice before them, accepted this cautiously outstretched official hand, and began constituting trades associations, a process half encouraged, half hampered, by the authorities.

When the great Exhibition of Modern Industry was opened in London in 1863, French workers were given facilities for visiting it, and a selected deputation duly came to England, half tourists, half representatives of the French proletariat, theoretically sent to the Exhibition in order to study the latest industrial developments. A meeting was arranged between them and the representative English unions. At this meeting, which originally was probably as vague in intention as other gatherings of its kind, there naturally arose such questions as comparative hours and wages in France and England, and the necessity of preventing employers from importing cheap black-leg labour from abroad with which to break strikes organized by local unions. A meeting was called in order to form an association which should be confined not merely to holding discussions and comparing notes, but for the purpose of beginning active economic and political co-operation, and perhaps for the promotion of an international democratic revolution. The initiative on this occasion came not from Marx, but from the English and French labour leaders themselves. On their fringe were radicals, of various kinds, Polish democrats, Italian Mazzinists, Proudhonists, Blanquists and neo-Jacobins from France and Belgium: anyone, indeed, who desired the fall of the existing order was at first freely welcomed.

The first meeting was held in St. Martin's Hall, and was presided over by Edward Beesly, a charming and benevolent figure, then professor of ancient history in the University of London, a radical and a positivist, who belonged to the small but notable group which included Frederic Harrison and Compton, and had been deeply influenced by Comte and the early French socialists. Its members could be counted on to support every enlightened measure, and, for many years alone among the educated men of their time defended the highly unpopular cause of trade unionism at a period when it was being denounced in the House of Commons as an instrument deliberately invented to foment ill will between the classes. The meeting resolved to constitute an international federation of working men, pledged not to reform but to destroy the prevalent system of economic relations, and to substitute in its place one in which the workers would themselves acquire the ownership of the means of production, which would put an end to their economic exploitation and cause the fruit of their labour to be communally shared, an end which entailed the ultimate abolition of private property in all its forms. Marx, who had previously held himself coldly aloof from other gatherings of democrats, perceived the solid character of this latest attempt at combination, organized as it was by genuine workers' representatives and advertising definite and concrete purposes in which his own influence was clearly traceable. He rarely took part in any movement which he had not initiated himself. This was to be the exception. The German artisans in London appointed him their representative on the executive committee, and by the time the second meeting was held to vote the constitution, he took entire charge of the proceedings. After the French and Italian delegates, to whom the task of drafting the statutes was entrusted, had failed to produce anything but the usual faded democratic commonplaces, Marx drew them up himself, adding an inaugural address which he composed for the occasion. The constitution which, as framed by the International Committee, was vague, humanitarian, and tinged with liberalism, emerged from his hands a tightly drawn, militant document constituting a rigorously disciplined body whose members were pledged to assist each other not merely in improving their common condition, but in systematically subverting, and whenever possible over-throwing, the existing capitalist régime by open political action, and in particular by gaining representation in democratic parliaments, as the followers of Lassalle were beginning to attempt to do in German countries. A formal request was thereupon made to include some expressions of respect for 'right and duty, truth, justice and freedom'. The words were inserted, but in a context in which Marx declared that 'they could do no possible harm'. The new constitution was passed, and Marx began to work with his customary feverish rapidity, emerging into the limelight of international activity after fifteen years, if not of obscurity, of inter-mittent light and darkness.

The Inaugural Address of the International is, after the Communist Manifesto, the most remarkable docu-ment of the Socialist Movement. It occupies little over a dozen octavo pages and opens with the declaration '. . . That the emancipation of the working class must be conquered by the working class themselves . . . that the economic subjection of the man of labour to the monopolizer of the means of labour . . . lies at the bottom of servitude in all its forms of social misery, mental degradation and political dependence. That the economic emancipation of the working class is therefore the great end to which every political movement ought to be subordinate as a means. That all efforts aiming at this great end have hitherto failed from want of solidarity between the manifold divisions of labour in each country, and from the absence of a fraternal bond of union between the working classes of different countries . . . for these means the undersigned . . . have taken the steps necessary for founding the International Working Men's Association.'

It contains a survey of the economic and social conditions of the working class from 1848, and contrasts the rapidly growing prosperity of the propertied classes with the depressed condition of the workers. 1848 is recognized as a crushing defeat for their class, yet even so it was not wholly without benefit: as a result of it, the feeling of international solidarity among workers had awoken. Its existence had made agitation for the legal limitation of the working day not entirely unsuccessful, this being the first definite victory over a policy of extreme *laissez-faire*. The co-operative movement had proved that high industrial efficiency was compatible with, and even increased by, the elimination of the capitalist slave-driver: wage labour had thus been demonstrated to be not a necessary but a transient and eradicable evil. The workers were at last beginning to grasp that they had nothing to gain and everything to lose by listening to their capitalist advisers who, whenever they could not use force, sought to play on national and religious prejudices, on personal or local interests, on the profound political ignorance of the masses. Whoever might gain by national or dynastic wars, it was the workers on both sides who always lost. Yet their strength was such that by common action they could prevent this exploitation in peace as in war: as, indeed, their success in intervening in England against the sending of help to the Southern states in the American civil war had proved. Against the formidable and in appearance overwhelming power of their enemy they had only one weapon—their numbers, 'but numbers weigh in the scales only when they are united and organized and led consciously towards a single aim'; it was in the political field that their slavery was most manifest. To hold aloof from politics in the name of economic organization, as Proudhon and Bakunin taught, was criminal short-sightedness; they would obtain justice only if they could uphold it, if necessary by force, wherever they saw it trampled upon. Even if they could not intervene with armed force, they could at least protest and demonstrate and harass their governments, until the supreme standards of morality and justice, by which relations between individuals were conventionally judged, became the laws governing relations between nations. But this could not be done without altering the existing economic structure of society which, in spite of minor improvements, necessarily worked for the degradation and enslavement of the working class. There was only one class in whose real interest it was to arrest this downward trend and remove the possibility of its occurrence: that was the class which, possessing nothing, was bound by no ties of interest or sentiment to the old world of injustice or misery—the class which was as much the invention of the new age as machinery itself. The Address ended like the *Communist Manifesto* with the words, 'Workers of the world unite!'

The tasks of the new organization as embodied in this document were: to establish close relations between the workers of various countries and trades; to collect relevant statistics; to inform the workers of one country of the conditions, needs and the plans of the workers of another; to discuss questions of common interest; to secure co-ordinated simultaneous action in all countries in the event of international crises; to publish regular reports on the work of the associations, and the like. It was to meet in annual congresses and would be convened by a democratically elected general council in which all affiliated countries would be represented. Marx left the constitution as elastic as possible in order to be able to include as many active workers' organizations as possible, however disparate their methods and character. At first he resolved to act cautiously and with moderation, to bind and unify, and eliminate dissidents gradually, as a greater measure of agreement was progressively reached. He carried out his policy precisely as he had planned it. The consequences were ruinous, although it is difficult to see what other tactics Marx could have adopted consistently with his principles.

The International grew rapidly. Union after union of workers in the principal countries of Europe was converted by the prospect of united warfare for higher wages, shorter hours and political representation: it was far better organized than either Chartism or the earlier communist leagues had ever been, partly because tactical lessons had been learnt. Independent activity on the part of individuals was suppressed, popular oratory was discouraged and rigid discipline in all departments was introduced, mainly because it was led and dominated by a single personality. The only man who might have attempted to rival Marx in the early years was Lassalle, and he was dead; even so, the spell of his legend was strong enough to insulate the Germans against full support of the London centre. Liebknecht, a man of mediocre talent, boundlessly devoted to Marx, preached the new creed with enthusiasm and skill, but the continuation of Bismarck's anti-socialist policy, and the tradition of nationalism derived from Lassalle, kept the German workers' activity within the frontiers of their country, preoccupied with problems of internal organization. As for Bakunin, that great disturber of men's spirits had lately returned to Western Europe after a romantic escape from Siberia, but while his personal prestige, both in the International and outside it, was immense, he had no organized following: he had drifted away from Herzen and the liberal agrarian party among the Russian *émigrés*, and no one knew whither he was tending, least of all he himself. In common with the great majority of Proudhonists he and his followers became members of the International, but since it was openly committed to political action, they did so in defiance of their principles. The most enthusiastic members at this time were English and French trade unionists, who were temporarily under the spell of the new experiment with its vast promise of prosperity and power; they were no theorists, nor wished to be, and left all such questions to the General Council of the International. While this mood lasted, Marx had no serious rivals in the organization, being altogether superior in intellect, revolutionary experience and strength of will, to the odd amalgam of professional men, factory workers and stray ideologists who, with the addition of one or two dubious adventurers, composed the First International Working Men's Association.

Marx was now forty-six years of age and in appearance and habits prematurely old. Of his six children three were dead, largely as a result of the material conditions of the life led by the family in their rooms in Soho: they had contrived to move to a more spacious house in Kentish Town, although they were still almost destitute. The great economic crisis, the severest yet experienced in Europe, which began in 1857, was warmly welcomed both by him and by Engels as likely to breed discontent and rebellion, but it also curtailed Engels's income, and so struck a blow at Marx himself at a moment when he could least afford it. The *New York Tribune* and occasional contributions to radical German newspapers saved him from literal starvation; but the margin by which the family survived was for twenty years perilously thin. By 1860 even the American source began to fail; the editor of the *New York Tribune*, Horace Greeley, a fervent supporter of democratic nationalism, found himself in growing disagreement with his European correspondent's sharply worded views. The economic crisis, and the added effect of the civil war, led to the dismissal of many of the *Tribune's* European correspondents: Dana pleaded to be allowed to retain Marx, but in vain. He was gradually edged out of his post during the beginning of 1861; the association finally ceased a year later. As for the International, it added to his duties and enlivened his existence, but did not increase his income. In despair he applied for a post of booking clerk in a railway office, but his tattered clothes and his menacing appearance were unlikely to produce a favourable impression on a potential employer of clerical labour, and his application was finally rejected on account of his illegible handwriting. It is difficult to see how, without the support of Engels, he and his family could have survived at all during those fearful years.

Meanwhile branches of the International had been established in Italy and Spain; by 1865 governments began to grow frightened; there was talk of arrests and proscriptions; the French Emperor made a half-hearted attempt to suppress it. This only served to heighten the fame and the prestige of the new body among the workers. For Marx, after the dark tunnel of the 'fifties, this was once more life and activity. The work of the International consumed his nights and days. With the customary devoted help of Engels he took personal possession of the central office, and acted not only as its semi-dictatorial adviser, but as the central drafting office and clearing-house of all correspondence. Everything passed through his hands and moved in the direction which he gave it. The French, a portion of the Swiss, to some degree the Belgian, and later the Italian sections, bred on the anti-authoritarianism of Proudhon and Bakunin, made vague but unavailing protests. Marx, who enjoyed complete ascendancy over the Council, tightened his hold still further : he insisted on rigid conformity to every point of the original programme. His old energy seemed to return. He wrote spirited, almost gay letters to Engels; even his theoretical works bear the imprint of this newly found vigour, and as often happens, intense work in one field stimulated dormant activity in another. A sketch of his economic theory had appeared in 1859 : but his major work, which poverty and ill-health had interrupted, now at last began to near its end.

Marx made few personal appearances at the meetings of the congress of the International: he preferred to control its activities from London, where he regularly attended the meetings of the General Council and issued detailed instructions to his followers on it. As always he trusted and relied almost entirely on Germans: he found a faithful mouthpiece in an elderly tailor named Eccarius, long resident in England, a man not burdened with excess of intelligence or imagination, but dependable and thorough. Eccarius, like the majority of Marx's underlings, eventually revolted, and joined the secessionists, but for eight years, as secretary to the Council of the International, he carried out Marx's instructions to the letter. Annual congresses were held in London, Geneva, Lausanne, Brussels, Basle, at which general problems were discussed and definite measures voted upon; common decisions were adopted with regard to hours and wages; such questions as the position of women and children, the type of political and economic pressure most suitable to differing conditions in various European countries, the possibility of collaboration with other bodies, were considered. Marx's chief concern was to arrive at a clear formulation of a concrete international policy in terms of specific demands coordinated with each other, and the creation of a rigorous discipline which guaranteed undeviating adhesion to this policy. He therefore successfully resisted all offers of alliance with such purely humanitarian bodies as the League of Peace and Freedom, then newly founded under the aegis of Mazzini, Bakunin and John Stuart Mill. This dictatorial policy was bound, sooner or later, to lead to discontent and rebellion; it crystallized round Bakunin whose conception of a loose federation of semi-independent local bodies began to gain adherents in the Swiss and Italian sections of the International, and to a lesser extent in France. Finally they resolved to constitute themselves, under Bakunin's leadership, into a body to be called the Democratic Alliance, affiliated to the International, but with an internal organization of its own pledged to resist centralization and to support federal autonomy. This was a heresy which even a more tolerant man than Marx could not afford to overlook: the International was not intended to be a mere correspondence society between a loose association of radical committees, but a unified political party pressing for a single end in all the centres of its dispersion. He believed firmly that any connexion with Bakunin—or indeed any Russian—was bound to end by badly betraying the working class, a view which he had acquired after his brief and enjoyable flirtation, and subsequent disillusionment, with the aristocratic Russian radicals of the 'forties. As for Bakunin, while he professed sincerely enough to admire Marx's personal genius, he never concealed either his personal antipathy for him, or his rooted loathing of Marx's belief in authoritarian methods, expressed both in his theories and in his practical organization of the revolutionary party.

'We, revolutionary anarchists', Bakunin declared, 'are the enemies of all forms of state and state organization . . . we think that all state rule, all governments, being by their very nature placed outside the mass of the people, must necessarily seek to subject it to customs and purposes entirely foreign to it. We therefore declare ourselves to be foes . . . of all state organizations as such, and believe that the people can only be happy and free, when, organized from below by means of its own autonomous and completely free associations, without the supervision of any guardians, it will create its own life.

'We believe power corrupts those who wield it as much as those who are forced to obey it. Under its corrosive influence, some become greedy and ambitious tyrants, exploiting society in their own interest, or in that of their class, while others are turned into abject slaves. Intellectuals, positivists, doctrinaires, all those who put science before life . . . defend the idea of the state and its authority as being the only possible salvation of society—quite logically, since from their false premiss that thought comes before life, that only abstract theory can form the starting-point of social practice . . . they draw the inevitable conclusion that since such theoretical knowledge is at present possessed by very few, these few must be put in control of social life, not only to inspire, but to direct all popular movements, and that no sooner is the revolution over than a new social organization must at once be set up; not a free association of popular bodies . . . working in accordance with the needs and instincts of the people, but a centralized dictatorial power concentrated in the hands of this academic minority, as if they really expressed the popular will. . . . The difference between such revolutionary dictatorship and the modern State is only one of external trappings. In substance both are a tyranny of the minority over the majority in the name of the people—in the name of the stupidity of the many and the superior wisdom of the few—and so they are equally reactionary, devising to secure political and economic privilege to the ruling minority, and the . . . enslavement of the masses, to destroy the present order only to erect their own rigid dictatorship on its ruins.'

Bakunin's attacks on Marx and Lassalle could not pass unnoticed, the more so because they were tinged by anti-semitism, for which his friend Herzen more than once had occasion to reproach him. And yet, when in 1869 Herzen begged him to leave the International, he wrote, with a characteristic burst of magnanimity, that he could not join the opponents of a man 'who has served [the cause of socialism] for twenty-five years with insight, energy, and disinterestedness in which he undoubtedly excelled us all'.

Marx's dislike of Bakunin did not blind him to the need for conceding a certain measure of regional inde-pendence for motives of sheer expediency. Thus he successfully foiled the plan to create international trade unions because he believed that this was premature and would lead to an immediate rift with the existing, nationally organized, trade unions from which, at any rate in England, the chief support of the International was drawn. But if he made this concession, he did so not for love of federalism as such, but solely not to endanger what had already been built up, without which he could not create a body, the existence of which would make the workers conscious that there were be-hind their demands, not, as in 1848, merely sympathizers here and there, prepared to offer moral support or at best occasional contributions—but a well-disciplined, militant force pledged to resist, and, when necessary, intimidate and coerce their own governments, unless justice were done to their brothers everywhere.

In order to create the permanent possibility of such active solidarity in theory and in practice, a central body in un-disputed authority, a kind of general staff responsible for strategy and tactics, seemed to him indispensable.

Bakunin, by his attempts to loosen the structure of the International and to encourage varieties of opinion in the local sections, appeared to him to be deliberately aiming to destroy this possibility. If he were successful, it would mean the loss of what had been won, a return to utopianism, the disappearance of the new sober outlook, of the realization that the sole strength of the workers lay in unity, that what delivered them into the hands of their enemies in 1848 was the fact that they were engaged in scattered risings, sporadic emotional outbursts of violence, instead of a single carefully concerted revolution, organized to begin at a moment chosen for its historical appropriateness, directed from a common source and to a common end, by men who had accurately studied the situation and their own and their enemy's strength. Bakuninism led to the dissipation of the revolutionary impulse, to the old romantic, noble, futile heroism, rich in saints and martyrs, but crushed only too easily by the more realistic enemy, and necessarily followed by a period of weakness and disillusionment likely to set the movement back for many decades. Marx did not under-estimate Bakunin's revolutionary energy and power to stir men's imaginations: indeed, it was for this reason that he regarded him as a dangerously disruptive force likely to breed chaos wherever he went. The workers' cause would rest on volcanic soil if he and his followers were allowed to irrupt into the ranks of its defenders. Hence after some years of desultory skirmishing, he decided upon an open attack. It ended with the excommunication of Bakunin and his followers from the ranks of the International.

CHAPTER X

'THE RED TERRORIST DOCTOR'

*We are what we are because of him: without him we should
still be sunk in a slough of confusion.*

FRIEDRICH ENGELS, 1883

THE first volume of *Das Kapital* was finally published
in 1867. The appearance of this book was an epoch-
making event in the history of international socialism
and in Marx's own life. It was conceived as a comprehensive treatise on the laws and morphology of the
economic organization of modern society, seeking
to describe the processes of production, exchange and
distribution as they actually occur, to explain their
present state as a particular stage in the development
constituted by the movement of the class struggle, in
Marx's own words, 'to discover the economic law of
motion of modern society' by establishing the natural
laws which govern the history of classes. The result
was a curious amalgam of economic theory, history,
sociology and propaganda which fits none of the
accepted categories. Marx certainly regarded it as
primarily a treatise on economic science. The earlier
economists, according to Marx, misunderstood the
nature of economic laws when they compared them
with the laws of physics and chemistry, and assumed
that, although social conditions may change, the laws
which govern them do not; with the result that their
systems either apply to imaginary worlds, peopled by
idealized economic men, modelled upon the writer's
own contemporaries, and therefore usually compounded

of characteristics which came into prominence only in the eighteenth and nineteenth centuries; or else describe societies which if they were ever real, have long since vanished. He therefore conceived it as his task to create a new system of concepts and definitions which should have definite application to the contemporary world, and be so constructed as to reflect the changing structure of economic life in relation not only to its past, but also to its future. In the first volume Marx made an attempt at once to provide a systematic exposition of certain basic theorems of economic science, and more specifically to describe the rise of the new industrial system, as a consequence of the new relations between employers and labour created by the effect of technological progress on the methods of production.

The first volume therefore deals with the productive process; that is, on the one hand, the relation between machinery and labour, and on the other between the actual producers, i.e. the workers and those who employ and direct them. The remaining volumes, published after his death by his executors, deal with the methods in use of marketing the finished product, i.e. the system of exchange and the financial machinery which it involves, and with relations between producers and consumers, which determine the rate of interest and profit.

The general thesis which runs through the entire work is that adumbrated in the *Communist Manifesto* and Marx's earlier economic writings.[1] It traces the rise of the modern proletariat by correlating it with the

[1] For a more detailed account of Marxist economic doctrine, together with the best-known criticisms of it, the reader is referred to the chapter on 'Communist Economics' in Professor H. J. Laski's *Communism*, published in this series.

general development of the technical means of production. When, in the course of their gradual evolution, these means become too costly and elaborate to be capable of being made by each man for his own use, certain individuals, owing to their superior skill, power and enterprise, or to accident of fortune, acquire sole control of such instruments and tools, and thus find themselves in a position in which they can hire the labour of others by offering them more in the form of a regular remuneration than they would receive as independent producers vainly attempting to achieve the same results with the old and obsolete tools which alone they have in their possession. As a result of selling their labour to others, these men themselves become so many commodities in the economic market, and their labour power acquires a definite price which fluctuates precisely like that of other commodities.

A commodity is any object embodying human labour for which there is a social demand. It is thus a concept which, he is careful to point out, can be applied only at a relatively late stage of social development: and is no more eternal than any other economic category. The commercial value of a commodity is assumed to be directly constituted by the number of hours of human labour which it takes an average producer to create an average specimen of its kind (a view derived from a somewhat similar doctrine held by Ricardo and the classical economists). A day's work by a labourer may well produce an object possessing a value greater than the value of the minimum quantity of commodities which he needs for his own support; he thus produces something more valuable than he consumes; indeed, unless he did so, his master would have no economic reason for employing him. As a commodity in the market, his labour power may itself be acquired for $£x$, which represents the minimum sum needed to maintain him in sufficient health to enable him to do his work efficiently; the goods he produces will sell for $£y$; $£y-x$ represents the extent by which he has increased the total wealth of society, and this is the residue which his employer pockets. Even after the reasonable reward of the employer's own work in his capacity as the organizer and manager of the processes of production and distribution is deducted, a definite residue of the social income remains, which in the form of rent, interest on investments, or commercial profit, is shared, according to Marx, not by society as a whole, but solely by those members of it who are called the capitalist or bourgeois class, distinguished from the rest by the fact that they alone in their capacity as sole owners of the means of production, obtain and accumulate such unearned increment.

Whether Marx's concept of value be interpreted as meaning the actual market price of commodities, or an average norm, round which the actual prices oscillate, or an ideal limit towards which they tend, or that which in a rationally organized society prices ought to be, or something more metaphysical and Hegelian, an impalpable essence, infused into brute matter by the creativeness of human labour, or, as unsympathetic critics have maintained, a confusion of all these; and again whether the notion of a uniform entity called undifferentiated human labour (which according to the theory constitutes economic value), different manifestations of which can be compared in respect of quantity alone, is, or is not, valid—and it is not easy to defend

Marx's use of either concept—the theory of exploitation based on them remains comparatively unaffected. The central thesis which made so powerful an appeal to workers, who did not for the most part begin to comprehend the intricacies of Marx's general argument about the relation of exchange value and actual prices, is that there is only one social class, their own, which produces more wealth than it enjoys, and that this residue is appropriated by other men simply by virtue of their strategical position as the sole possessors of the means of production, that is, natural resources, machinery, means of transport, financial credit, and so forth; for without these the workers cannot create; while control over them gives those who have it the power of starving the rest of mankind into capitulation on their own terms.

Political, social, religious and legal institutions are represented as being so many moral and intellectual weapons designed to organize the world in the interest of the employers. These last employ, over and above the producers of commodities, that is, the proletariat, a whole army of ideologists: propagandists, interpreters and apologists, who defend the capitalist system, embellish it, and create literary and artistic monuments to it, designed to increase the confidence and optimism of those who benefit under it, and make it appear more palatable to its victims. But if the development of technology, as Saint-Simon correctly discovered, has for a period given this unique power to landowners, industrialists and financiers—every type of middleman, its uncontrollable advance will no less inevitably destroy them.

Already Fourier, and after him Proudhon, had declaimed against the processes by which the great bankers and manufacturers, by means of their superior resources, tend to eliminate small traders and craftsmen from the economic market, creating a mass of discontented, *déclassé* individuals, who are automatically forced into the ranks of the proletariat. Ruthless competition between individual capitalists, seeking to increase the quantity of surplus value, and the natural necessity arising from this of lowering the cost of production and finding new markets, is bound to lead to greater and greater fusion of rival firms, that is to a ceaseless process of amalgamation, until only the largest and most powerful groups are left in existence, all others being forced into a position of dependence or semi-dependence, in the new centralized industrial hierarchy, which grows, and will continue to grow, faster and faster. Centralization is a direct product of rationalization: of increased efficiency in production and transport secured by the pooling of resources, of the formation of great monopolistic trusts and combines which are capable of planned co-ordination. The workers previously scattered among many small enterprises, reinforced by continual influx of the sons and daughters of the ruined small traders and manufacturers, automatically become united into a single self-conscious proletarian army by the very processes of integration at work among their masters. Their power as a political and economic force grows correspondingly greater. Already trade unions, developing in the shadow of the factory system, represent a far more powerful weapon in the hands of the proletariat than any that existed before. The process of industrial expansion will tend to organize society more and more into the shape of an immense pyramid, with fewer and increasingly powerful capitalists at its summit and a vast, discontented mass of exploited workers and colonial slaves forming its base. The more machinery replaces human labour the lower the rate of profit is bound to fall, since 'surplus value' is determined solely by the quantity of the latter. The struggle between competing capitalists and their countries, which are in effect controlled by them, will grow bitterer and more deadly, being wedded to a system of unhampered competition, under which each can only survive by overreaching and destroying his rivals.

Within the framework of capitalism and unchecked private enterprise, these processes cannot be controlled, since the vested interests on which capitalist society rests, depend for their survival on absolute freedom of competition. Marx did not, however, clearly foresee the consequences of the competition between rival imperialisms, and, in particular, the development of political nationalism as a force cutting across and transforming the development of capitalism itself, and offering a bulwark to the gradually impoverished section of the *bourgeoisie*, which forms an alliance with the reaction in its desperate anxiety to avoid its Marxist destiny of falling into the proletariat below it.

His classification of social strata into the obsolescent military-feudal aristocracy, the industrial *bourgeoisie*, the *petite bourgeoisie*, the proletariat, and that casual riff-raff on the edge of society which he called the *Lumpenproletariat*—a fruitful and original classification for its time—over-simplifies issues when it is too mechanically applied to the twentieth century. A more elaborate instrument is required, if only to deal with the independent behaviour of classes, like the semi-ruined *petite bourgeoisie,* the growing salaried lower middle class, and above all the vast agricultural population, classes which Marx regarded as naturally reactionary, but forced by their growing pauperization either to sink to the level of the proletariat, or to offer their services as mercenaries to its protagonist, the industrial *bourgeoisie.* The history of post-war Europe, at any rate in the West, requires to be considerably distorted before it can be made to fit this hypothesis.

Marx prophesied that the periodic crises due to the absence of planned economies, and unchecked industrial strife, would necessarily grow more frequent and acute. Wars, on a hitherto unprecedented scale, would ravage the civilized world, until finally the Hegelian contradictions of a system, whose continuance depends upon more and more destructive conflicts between its constituent parts, would obtain a violent solution. The ever-decreasing group of capitalists in power would be overthrown by the workers whom they themselves would have so efficiently drilled into a compact, disciplined body. With the disappearance of the last possessing class, the final end would be reached of the war between the classes, which is the sole and sufficient cause of economic scarcity and social strife.

In a celebrated passage in the twenty-second chapter of the first volume of *Das Kapital* he declared: 'While there is a progressive diminution in the number of capitalist magnates, there is of course a corresponding increase in the mass of poverty, enslavement, degeneration and exploitation, but at the same time there is a steady intensification of the role of the working class—a class which grows ever more numerous, and is disciplined, unified and organized by the very mechanism of the capitalist method of production which has flourished with it and under it. The centralization of the means of production and the socialization of labour reach a point where they prove incompatible with their capitalist husk. This bursts asunder. The knell of private property sounds. The expropriators are expropriated.' The State, the instrument whereby the authority of the ruling class is artificially enforced, having lost its function, will disappear; the ideal community, painted in colours at once too simple and too fantastic by the Utopians of the past, will at last be reached—a community in which there will be neither master nor slave, neither rich nor poor, in which the world's goods, being produced in accordance with social demand unhampered by the caprice of individuals, will be distributed not indeed equally—a notion so lamely borrowed by the workers from the liberal ideologists with their utilitarian concept of justice as arithmetical equality—but rationally, that is unequally: for, as a man's capacities and needs are unequal, his reward, if it is to be just, must, in the formula of the *Communist Manifesto*, accrue 'to every one according to his need, from every one according to his capacity'. Men, emancipated at last from the tyranny both of nature and of their own ill-adapted and ill-controlled, and therefore oppressive institutions, will begin to develop their capacities to the fullest extent. True freedom, so obscurely adumbrated by Hegel, will be realized. Human history in the true sense will only then begin.

The publication of *Das Kapital* had at last provided a definite intellectual foundation for international socialism in the place of a scattered mass of vaguely defined and conflicting ideas. The interdependence of the

historical economic and political theses preached by
Marx and Engels was revealed in this monumental
compilation. It became the central objective of attack
and defence. All subsequent forms of socialism hereafter
defined themselves in terms of their attitude to the position taken in it, and were understood and classified by
their resemblance to it. After a brief period of obscurity,
its fame began to grow and reached an extraordinary
height. It acquired a symbolic significance beyond
anything written since the age of faith. It has been
blindly worshipped, and blindly hated, by millions who
have not read a line of it, or have read without understanding its obscure and tortuous prose. In its name
revolutions were made; the counter-revolutions which
followed concentrated upon its suppression as the most
potent and insidious of the enemy's weapons. A new
social order has been established which professes its
principles and sees in it the final and unalterable expression of its faith. It has called into existence an army
of interpreters and casuists, whose unceasing labours
for nearly three-quarters of a century have buried it
beneath a mountain of commentary, which has out-
grown in influence the sacred text itself.

In Marx's own life it marked a decisive moment.
He intended it to be his greatest contribution to the
emancipation of humanity, and had sacrificed to it
fifteen years of his life and much of his public ambition.
The labour which had gone towards it was truly prodigious. For its sake he endured poverty, illness and
persecution both public and personal, suffering these
not gladly indeed, but with a single-minded stoicism
whose strength and harshness both moved and frightened
those who came in contact with it.

He offered to dedicate his book to Darwin, for whom he had a greater intellectual admiration than for any other of his contemporaries, regarding him as having, by his theory of evolution and natural selection, done for the morphology of the natural sciences, what he himself was striving to do for human history. Darwin hastily declined the honour in a polite, cautiously phrased letter, saying that he was unhappily ignorant of economic science, but offered the author his good wishes in what he assumed to be their common end—the advancement of human knowledge. It was dedicated to the memory of Wilhelm Wolff, a Silesian communist, who had been his devoted follower since 1848, and had recently died in Manchester. The published volume was the first part of the projected work, the rest was still a confused mass of notes, references and sketches. He sent copies of it to his old associates, to Freiligrath who congratulated him on having produced a useful work of reference, and to Feuerbach who said that he found it 'rich in undeniable facts of the most interesting, but at the same time most horrible nature'. Ruge gave it more discriminating praise; it obtained at least one critical notice in England, in the *Saturday Review*, which quaintly observed that 'the presentation of the subject invests the driest economic questions with certain peculiar charm'. It was more widely noticed in Germany where Marx's friends Liebknecht and Kugelmann, a Hanover physician who had conceived an immense admiration for him, made vigorous propaganda for it. In particular Joseph Dietzgen, a self-taught German cobbler in St. Petersburg, who became one of Marx's most ardent disciples, did much to popularize it with the German masses.

Marx's scientific appetite had not diminished since his Paris days. He believed in exact scholarship and sternly drove his reluctant followers into the reading-room of the British Museum. Liebknecht, in his memoirs, describes how day after day the 'scum of international communism' might be seen meekly seated at the desks in the reading-room, under the eye of the master himself. Indeed no social or political movement has laid such emphasis on research and erudition. The extent of Marx's own reading is to some degree indicated by the references in his works alone, which explore exceedingly obscure by-ways in ancient, medieval, and modern literature. The text is liberally sprinkled with footnotes, long, mordant and annihilating, which recall Gibbon's classical employment of this weapon. The adversaries at whom they are directed are for the most part for-gotten names to-day, but occasionally his shafts are aimed at well-known figures; Macaulay, Gladstone, and one or two notorious academic economists of the time, are attacked with a savage concentration which has inaugurated a new epoch in the technique of public vituperation, and created the school of socialist polemical writing which has entirely altered the general character of political controversy. There is conspicuously little praise in the book. The warmest tribute is earned by the British factory inspectors, whose fearless and un-biased reports both of the appalling conditions which they witnessed, and of the means adopted by factory owners to circumvent the law, is declared to be a uniquely honourable phenomenon in the history of bourgeois society. The technique of social research was revolutionized by the example set by him in the use of Blue Books and official reports: the greater part of his detailed indictment of modern industrialism is based almost wholly upon them.

After his death, Engels, who edited the second and third volumes of *Das Kapital*, found the manuscript in a far more chaotic condition than he expected. The year in which the first volume appeared marks not a turning but a breaking-point in Marx's life. His views during the remaining sixteen years of his life altered little; he added, revised, corrected, wrote pamphlets and letters, but published nothing that was new; he reiterated the old position tirelessly, but the tone is milder, a faint note almost of querulous self-pity, totally absent before, is now discernible. His belief in the proximity, even in the ultimate inevitability of a world revolution, diminished. His prophecies had been disappointed too often; he had confidently predicted a great upheaval in 1842, during a weavers' rising in Silesia, and even inspired Heine to write his famous poem upon it which he published in his Paris journal; again in 1851, 1857 and 1872 he expected revolutionary outbreaks which failed to materialize. His long-term predictions were far more successful, not only with regard to the general development of capitalism—concerning which he has proved a singularly true prophet, erring only in supposing that centralization of control neces-sarily entailed centralization of ownership of economic resources, a hypothesis not borne out by the growth in the number of small investors, and the increasing tendency to divide the land into small holdings—but also more specifically, as when, after the annexation of Alsace-Lorraine by Prussia, he foretold that this would throw France into the arms of Russia and so bring about the first great world war. He allowed that the revolution may be longer in arriving than he and Engels had once estimated, and in some countries, notably in England, where in his day there was no real army and no real bureaucracy, it may actually not occur at all, 'although', he enigmatically added, 'history indicates otherwise'. He was not fifty when he began to subside into conscious old age. The heroic period was over.

Das Kapital created a new reputation for its author. His previous books had been passed over in silence even in German-speaking countries: his new work was reviewed and discussed as far afield as Russia and Spain. In the next ten years it was translated into French, English, Russian, Italian: indeed, Bakunin himself gallantly offered to translate it into Russian. But this project, if it was ever begun, collapsed in circumstances of sordid personal and financial scandal which were partly responsible for the demise of the International five years later. Its sudden rise to fame was due to a major event which two years earlier altered the history of Europe and completely changed the direction in which the working class movement had hitherto developed.

If Marx and Engels sometimes predicted events which failed to happen, they more than once failed to foresee events which did. Thus Marx denied that the Crimean War would occur, and backed the wrong side in the Austro-Prussian War. The Franco-Prussian War of 1870 came to them as something wholly unexpected. For years they had underestimated Prussian strength; the true alliance of cynicism and brute force was in their eyes represented by the Emperor of the French. Bismarck was an able Junker, who served his King and his class; even his victory over Austria did not convince them of his real quality or aims. Marx may have been genuinely deceived to some extent by Bismarck's representation of the war as being on his part purely defensive, for he signed the protest which the Council of the International immediately published only after it had been altered to make this clear—a step for which many socialists in Latin countries never forgave him, insisting in later years that it was inspired by pure German patriotism, to which both he and Engels were always conspicuously prone. The International in general, and in particular its German members, behaved irreproachably throughout the brief campaign. The Council in its proclamation, issued in the middle of the war, warned the German workers against supporting the policy of annexation which Bismarck might well pursue; it explained in clear terms that the interests of the French and German proletariat were identical, being menaced only by the common enemy, the capitalist bourgeoisie of both countries, which had brought about the war for its own ends, wasting for their sakes the lives and substance of the working class equally of Germany and of France. In due course it exhorted the French workers to support the formation of a republic on a broadly democratic basis. During the wild wave of war chauvinism which swept over Germany, and engulfed even the left wing of the Lassallians, only the Marxists, Liebknecht and Bebel, preserved their sanity. To the indignation of the entire country they abstained from voting for war credits and spoke vigorously in the Reichstag against the war, and in particular against the annexation of Alsace-Lorraine. For this they were charged with treason and imprisoned. In a celebrated letter to Engels, Marx pointed out that the defeat of Germany, which would have strengthened Bonapartism and crippled the German workers for many years to come, might have been even more disastrous than German victory. By transferring the centre of gravity from Paris to Berlin, Bismarck was doing their work for them, however unconsciously; for the German workers, being better organized and better disciplined than the French, were consequently a stronger citadel of social democracy than Frenchmen could have been; while the defeat of Bonapartism would remove a nightmare from Europe.

In the autumn the French army was defeated at Sédan, the Emperor taken prisoner, and Paris besieged. The King of Prussia, who had solemnly sworn that the war was defensive and directed not against France but against Napoleon, changed his tactics, and, armed with an enthusiastic plebiscite from his people, demanded the cession of Alsace-Lorraine and the payment of an indemnity of five billion francs. The tide of English opinion, hitherto anti-Bonapartist and pro-German, under the influence of continual reports of Prussian atrocities in France, veered round sharply. The International issued a second Manifesto violently protesting against the annexation, denouncing the dynastic ambitions of the Prussian King, and calling upon the French workers to unite with all defenders of democracy against the common Prussian foe. 'If frontiers are to be fixed by military interests', wrote Marx in 1870, 'there will be no end of claims, because every military line is necessarily faulty and may be improved by annexing some more outlying territory: they can never be fixed fairly or finally because they always must be improved by the conqueror or the conquered, and consequently carry within them the seeds of fresh wars. History will measure its retribution, not by the extent of square miles conquered from France, but by the intensity of the crime of reviving, in the second half of the nineteenth century, *the policy of conquest.*' This time war credits were voted against, not by Liebknecht and Bebel alone, but also by the Lassallians, shamed out of their recent patriotism. Marx jubilantly wrote to Engels that for the first time the principles and policy of the International had obtained public expression in a European legislative assembly: the International had become a force to be officially reckoned with: the dream of a united proletarian party with identical ends in all countries was beginning to be realized. Paris was presently starved into submission and capitulated; a national assembly was elected, Thiers was made President of the new Republic, and appointed a provisional government of conservative views. In March the government made an attempt to disarm the Paris National Guard, a volunteer citizen force which showed signs of radical sympathies. It refused to give up its arms, declared its autonomy, deposed the officials of the provisional government, and elected a revolutionary committee of the people as the true government of France. The regular troops were brought to Versailles and invested the rebellious city. It was the first campaign of what both sides immediately recognized to be an open class war.

The Commune, as the new government described itself, was neither created nor inspired by the International: it was not even, in a strict sense, socialist in its doctrines, unless a dictatorship of any popularly elected committee in itself constitutes a socialist phenomenon. It consisted of a highly heterogeneous collection of individuals, for the most part followers of Blanqui,

Proudhon, and Bakunin, with an admixture of pure rhetoricians, like Félix Pyat, who knew only that they were fighting for France, the people, and the revolution, and proclaimed death to all tyrants, priests and Prussians. Workmen, soldiers, writers, painters like Courbet, scholars like the geographer Elisée Réclus and the critic Vallès, ambiguous politicians like Rochefort, foreign exiles of mildly liberal views, bohemians and adventurers of every description were swept up in a common revolutionary wave. It rose at a moment of national hysteria after the moral and material misery of a siege and a capitulation, at a moment when the national revolution which promised to do away finally with the last relics of Bonapartist and Orleanist reaction, denounced by Thiers and his ministers, abandoned by the middle classes, uncertain of support among the peasantry, seemed suddenly threatened with the return of all that it most feared and loathed, the generals, the financiers, the priests. By a great effort the people had shaken off the nightmare first of the Empire, then of the siege; they had hardly awoken yet when the spectres seemed to advance upon them once again: terrified, they revolted. This common sense of horror before the resurgence of the past was almost the sole bond which united the Communards. Their views on political organization were vague to a degree: they announced that the state in its old form was abolished, and called upon the people in arms to govern itself.

Presently, as supplies began to give out, and the condition of the besieged grew more desperate, terror developed: proscriptions began, men and women were condemned and executed, many of them certainly guiltless, and few deserving of death. Among those executed was the Archbishop of Paris who had been held as a hostage against the army at Versailles. The rest of Europe watched the monstrous events with growing indignation and disgust. The Communards seemed even to enlightened opinion, even to old and tried friends of the people like Louis Blanc and Mazzini, to be a band of criminal lunatics dead to the appeal of humanity, social incendiaries pledged to destroy all religion and all morality, men driven out of their minds by real and imaginary wrongs, scarcely responsible for their enormities. Practically the entire European Press, reactionary and liberal alike, combined to give the same impression. Here and there a radical journal condemned less roundly than the others, and timidly pleaded extenuating circumstances. The atrocities of the Commune did not long remain unavenged. The retribution which the victorious army exacted took the form of mass executions; the white terror, as is common in such cases, far outdid in acts of bestial cruelty the worst excesses of the régime, the misdeeds of which it had come to end.

The International vacillated; composed as it largely was of enemies of the Blanquists and neo-Jacobins who formed the majority of the Commune, opposed to the Communard programme, and in particular to acts of terrorism, it had, moreover, formally advised against the revolt declaring that 'any attempt at upsetting the new government in the present crisis, . . . would be desperate folly'. The English members were particularly anxious not to compromise themselves by open association with a body which, in the opinion of the majority of their countrymen, was little better than a gang of common murderers. Marx solved their doubts by a very characteristic act. In the name of the International he published an address in which he proclaimed that the moment for analysis and criticism had passed. After giving a swift and vivid account of the events which led to the creation of the Commune, of its rise and fall, he acclaimed it as the first open and defiant manifestation in history of the strength and idealism of the working class—the first pitched battle which it had fought against its oppressors before the eyes of the whole world, an act forcing all its false friends, the radical bourgeoisie, the democrats and humanitarians to show themselves in their true colours, as enemies to the ultimate ends for which it was prepared to live and die. He went further than this: he recognized the Commune as that transitional form of social structure by passing through which alone the workers could gain their ultimate emancipation. To this extent he once more, as in 1850 and 1852, retracted the doctrine of the *Communist Manifesto*, which had asserted, as against the French utopians and early anarchists, that the immediate end of the revolution was not to destroy, but to seize the state and make use of it to liquidate the enemy.

His pamphlet, later entitled *The Civil War in France*, was not primarily intended as a historical study: it was a tactical move, and one of typical audacity and intransigeance. Marx was sometimes blamed by his own followers for allowing the International to be linked in the popular mind with a band of law-breakers and assassins, an association which earned for it an unnecessarily sinister reputation. This was not the kind of consideration which could have influenced him in the slightest degree. He was, all his life, a convinced and uncompromising believer in a violent working class revolution. The Commune was the first spontaneous rising of the workers in their capacity as workers: the June *émeute* of 1848, was, in his view, an attack on, and not by, them. The Commune was not directly inspired by Marx. He regarded it, indeed, as a political blunder: his adversaries the Blanquists and Proudhonists predominated in it to the end; and yet its significance in his eyes was immense. Before it there had indeed been many scattered streams of socialist thought and action; but this rising, with its world repercussions, the great effect which it was bound to have upon the workers of all lands, was the first event of the new era. The men who had died in it and for it, were the first martyrs of international socialism, their blood would be the seed of the new proletarian faith: whatever the tragic faults and shortcomings of the Communards, they were as nothing before the magnitude of the historical role which these men had played, the position which they were destined to occupy in the tradition of proletarian revolution.

By coming forward to pay them open homage he achieved what he intended to achieve: he helped to create a heroic legend of socialism. More than thirty years later Lenin defended the Moscow rising, which occurred during the abortive Russian revolution of 1905, against the highly damaging criticisms of Plekhanov, by quoting the attitude of Marx towards the Commune: by pointing out that the emotional and symbolic value of the memory of a great heroic outburst, however ill conceived, however harmful in its immediate results, was an infinitely greater and more permanent asset to a revolutionary movement than the realization of its futility at a moment when what matters most is not to write accurate history, or even to learn its lessons, but to make it.

The publication of the address embarrassed and shocked many members of the International and hastened its ultimate dissolution. Marx attempted to forestall all reproaches by revealing his name as the sole author of the work. 'The Red Terrorist Doctor', as he was now popularly known, became overnight the object of public odium: anonymous letters began to arrive, his life was several times threatened. Jubilantly he wrote to Engels: 'It is doing me good after twenty long and boring years of idyllic isolation like a frog in a swamp. The Government organ—the *Observer*—is even threatening me with prosecution. Let them try it. I snap my fingers at the canaille!' The hubbub died down, but the damage done to the International was permanent: it became indissolubly connected in the minds both of the police and of the general public with the outrages of the Commune. A blow was dealt to the alliance of the English trade-union leaders with the International, which was, in any case, from their point of view entirely opportunist, based on its usefulness in promoting specific union interests. The unions were at this time being strongly wooed by the Liberal Party with promises of support upon these very issues. The prospect of a peaceful and respectable conquest of power made them less than ever anxious to be associated with a notorious revolutionary conspiracy; their sole end was to raise the standard of living and the social and political status of the skilled workers whom they represented. They did not look upon themselves as a political party, and if they subscribed to the programme of the International, this was due partly to the elasticity of its statutes, which skilfully avoided committing its members to definitely revolutionary ends, but most of all to their haziness on political issues. This fact was well appreciated by the Government which, in reply to a circular from the Spanish Government demanding the suppression of the International, replied in the person of the Foreign Secretary, Lord Granville, that in England they felt no danger of armed insurrection: the English members were peaceful men, solely occupied in labour negotiations, and gave the Government no ground for apprehension. Marx himself was bitterly aware of the truth of this: even Harney and Jones were in his eyes preferable to the men he now had to deal with, solid trade-union officials like Odger, or Cremer or Applegarth, who distrusted foreigners, cared little for events outside their country, and took little interest in ideas.

No meetings of the International having been held in 1870-1, a meeting was convened in London in 1872. The most important proposal brought up by this Congress, that the working class henceforth cease to rely in the political struggle upon the assistance of bourgeois parties, and form a party of their own, was, after a stormy debate, carried by the votes of the English delegates. The new political party was not set up during Marx's lifetime, but, in idea at least, the Labour party was born at this meeting, and may be regarded as Marx's greatest single contribution to the internal history of his adopted land. At the same congress the English delegates insisted on, and won, the right to form a separate local organization instead of, as before, being represented by the General Council. This displeased and frightened Marx: it was a gesture of distrust, almost of rebellion; at once he suspected the machinations of Bakunin, whom the recent events in France had put in a proud and ecstatic mood, since he felt that they were overwhelmingly due to his personal influence. A large part of Paris was destroyed by fire during the Commune: this fire seemed to him a symbol of his own life, and a magnificent realization of his favourite paradox: 'Destruction, too, is a kind of creation.'

Marx neither understood nor wished to understand the emotional basis of Bakunin's acts and declarations: his influence was a menace to the movement, and must consequently be destroyed.

'The International was founded', he wrote in 1871, 'in order to replace the socialist and semi-socialist sects with a genuine organization of the working class for its struggle. . . . Socialist sectarianism and a real working-class movement are in inverse ratio to each other. Sects have a right to exist only so long as the working class is not mature enough to have an independent movement of its own: as soon as that moment arrives sectarianism becomes reactionary. . . . The history of the International is a ceaseless battle of the General Council against dilettantist experiments and sects. . . . Towards the end of 1868 the International was joined by Bakunin whose purpose it was to create an International within the International, and to place himself at its head. For M. Bakunin, his doctrine (an absurd patchwork composed of bits and pieces of views taken from Proudhon, Saint-Simon, &c.) was, and still is, something of secondary importance, serving him only as a means of acquiring personal influence and power. But if Bakunin, as a theoriest, is nothing, Bakunin, the intriguer, has attained to the highest peak

of his profession. . . . As for his political non-participation, every movement in which the working class as
such is opposed to the ruling classes, and exercises
pressure upon it from without, is *eo ipso* a political
movement . . . but when the workers' organization is
not so highly developed that it can afford to risk decisive
engagement with the dominant political power—then it
must be prepared for this by ceaseless agitation against
the crimes and follies of the ruling class. Otherwise it
becomes a plaything in its hands, as was demonstrated
by the September revolution in France, and, to some
extent, by the recent successes in England of Gladstone
& Co.'

Bakunin at this period had entered upon the last and
strangest phase of his bizarre existence. He had completely fallen under the spell of a young Russian terrorist,
Nechayev, whose audacity and freedom from scruple
he found irresistible. Nechayev, who believed in black-
mail and intimidation as essential revolutionary weapons
justified by their end, had written an anonymous letter
to the agent of the prospective publisher of Bakunin's
Russian version of *Das Kapital*, threatening him in
general but violent terms, if he should continue to force
his wretched hackwork upon men of genius, or pester
Bakunin for the return of the advance which had been
paid him. The frightened and infuriated agent sent the
letter to Marx. It is doubtful whether the evidence of
the intrigues conducted by Bakunin's organization, the
Democratic Alliance, would in itself have been sufficient
to secure his expulsion, since he numbered many personal supporters at the Congress; but the report of the
committee instructed to look into this scandal and the
dramatic production of the Nechayev letter, turned the

scale. After long and stormy sessions, in the course of which even the Proudhonists had finally been persuaded that no party could preserve its unity while Bakunin was in its ranks, he and his closest associates were expelled by a small majority.

Marx's next proposal also came as a bombshell to the uninitiated members of the Congress: it was to transfer the seat of the Council to the United States. Everyone realized that this was tantamount to the dissolution of the International. America was not merely infinitely distant from European affairs, but insignificant in the affairs of the International. The French delegates declared that one might as well remove it to the moon. Marx gave no explicit reason for this proposal, which was formally moved by Engels, but its purpose must have been clear enough to all those present. He could not operate without the loyal and unquestioned obedience of at least some sections of the body over which he ruled: England had seceded; he had thought of moving the Council to Belgium, but there, too, the anti-Marxist element was becoming formidable; in Germany the government would suppress it; France, Switzerland and Holland were far from reliable; Italy and Spain were definitely Bakuninist strongholds. Sooner than face a bitter struggle which could end at best in a Pyrrhic victory and destroy all hope of a proletarian unity for many generations, Marx decided, after ensuring that it did not fall into Bakuninists' hands, to allow the International to die peacefully.

His enemies claim that he judged the merit of all socialist assemblies solely by the degree to which he was himself permitted to control them: this equation was certainly made both by him and by Engels and made quite automatically; neither ever showed any sign of understanding the bewildered indignation which this attitude excited among broad sections of their followers. Marx attended the Hague congress in person, and his prestige was such that, in spite of violent opposition, the Congress finally by a narrow majority voted its own virtual extinction. Its later meetings were sordid travesties: it finally expired in Philadelphia in 1876. The International was, indeed, reconstituted thirty years later, but by that time—a period of rapidly increasing Socialist activity in all countries—its character was very different. Despite its explicitly revolutionary aims, it was more parliamentary, more respectable, more optimistic, essentially conciliatory in temper, more than half committed to the belief in the inevitability of the gradual evolution of capitalist society into moderate socialism under persistent but peaceful pressure from below.

CHAPTER XI

LAST YEARS

I remarked [to Marx] that as I grew older I became more tolerant. 'Do you', he said, '*do* you?'
H. M. HYNDMAN, *Record of an Adventurous Life*

THE duel with Bakunin is the last public episode in Marx's life. The revolution seemed dead everywhere, although its embers glowed faintly in Russia and Spain. The reaction was once more triumphant, in a milder form, indeed, than in the days of his youth, prepared to make definite concessions to its adversary, but appearing to possess all the more stability for that reason. The peaceful conquest of political and economic control seemed the workers' best hope of emancipation. The prestige of Lassalle's followers in Germany rose steadily, and Liebknecht, who represented the Marxist opposition, now that the International was dead, was inclined to come to terms with them, in order to form a single united party. He was persuaded that placed as he was inside Germany, he had a better grasp of the tactical exigencies than Marx and Engels, who continued to live in England and would not listen to any suggestion of compromise. The two parties finally held a conference at Gotha in 1875 and formed an alliance, issuing a common programme composed by the leaders of both factions. It was naturally submitted to Marx for approval. He left no doubt as to the impression which it made on him.

A violently worded attack was instantly dispatched to Liebknecht in Berlin and Engels was commanded to write in a similar strain. Marx accused his disciples of

straying into the use of the misleading, half-meaning-
less terminology inherited from Lassalle and the True
Socialists, interspersed with vague liberal phrases which
he had spent half his life in exposing and eliminating.
The programme itself seemed to him to be permeated
by the spirit of compromise and to rest on a belief in
the possibility of attaining social justice by peacefully
agitating for such trivial ends as a 'just' remuneration
for labour, and the abolition of the law of inheritance—
Proudhonist and Saint-Simonian remedies for this or that
abuse, calculated to prop up the capitalist system rather
than hasten its collapse. In the form of angry marginal
notes he conveyed for the last time his own conception
of what the programme of a militant socialist party
ought to be. The loyal Liebknecht received this, as
everything else which came from London, meekly, and
even reverently, but made no use of it. The alliance
continued and grew in strength. Two years later Liebknecht was again sharply criticized by Engels, who took
an even lower view than Marx of his political capacity.
On this occasion the cause was the appearance in the
pages of the official organ of the German Social Democratic party of articles by, and in support of, a certain
Eugen Dühring, a radical lecturer on economics in the
University of Berlin, a man of violently anti-capitalist
but hardly socialist views, who was acquiring growing
influence in the ranks of the German party. Against
him Engels published his longest and most comprehensive work, the last written in collaboration with Marx;
it contained an authoritative version of the materialist
view of history, expounded in the blunt, vigorous, lucid
prose which Engels wrote with great facility. *The Anti-
Dühring*, as it came to be called, is an attack on the

undialectical, positivistic materialism, then increasingly popular among scientific writers and journalists, which maintained that all natural phenomena could be interpreted in terms of the motion of matter in space, and advances against it the principle of the universal working of the dialectical principle far beyond the categories of human history, in the realms of biology, physics and mathematics. Engels was a versatile and well-read man, and had, by sheer industry, acquired some rudimentary knowledge of these subjects, but his discussions of them are exceedingly unfortunate. In particular the over-ambitious attempt to discover the working of the triad of the Hegelian dialectic in the mathematical rule by which the product of two negative quantities is positive, has proved a source of much embarrassment to later Marxists, who have found themselves saddled with the impossible task of defending an eccentric view not entailed by anything that Marx himself had ever asserted at any rate in his published writings. Marxist mathematics of our own day is a subject which, like Cartesian physics, forms a peculiar and isolated enclave in the development of a great intellectual movement, of antiquarian rather than scientific interest. Perhaps when Marx, towards the end of his life, declared that whatever else he might be, he was certainly not a Marxist, he had such extravagances in view. Very different are the chapters later reprinted as a pamphlet under the title *The Evolution from Utopian to Scientific Socialism.* That is written in Engels's best vein, and gives an account of the growth of Marxism from its origins in German idealism, French political theory and English economic science. It is still the best brief autobiographical appreciation of Marxism by one of its creators, hardly surpassed even in the works of the most brilliant and many-sided of all later writers on Marxism, the Russian publicist Plekhanov.

The attack on the Gotha Programme was Marx's last violent intervention in the affairs of the party. No similar crisis occurred again in his lifetime, and he was left free to devote his remaining years to theoretical studies and vain attempts to restore his failing health. He had moved from Kentish Town first to one, then to another home on Haverstock Hill, not far from Engels, who had sold his share in the family business to his partner, and had established himself in London in a large, commodious house in St. John's Wood. A year or two before this he had settled a permanent annuity on Marx, which, modest though it was, enabled him to pursue his work in peace. They saw each other nearly every day, and together carried on an immense correspondence with socialists in every land, by many of whom they had come to be regarded with increasing respect and veneration. Marx was now without question the supreme moral and intellectual authority of international socialism; Lassalle and Proudhon had died in the 'sixties, Bakunin, in poverty and neglect, in 1876. The death of his great enemy evoked no public comment from Marx: perhaps because his harsh obituary notice of Proudhon in a German newspaper had caused a wave of indignation among the French socialists, and he thought it more tactful to remain silent. His sentiments towards his adversaries, living and dead, had not altered, but he was physically less capable of the active campaigns of his youth and middle years; overwork and a life of poverty had finally undermined his strength; he was tired, and often ill, and began to be preoccupied

by his health. Every year, generally accompanied by
his younger daughter Eleanor, he would visit the
English seaside, or a German or Bohemian spa, where
he would occasionally meet old friends and followers,
who sometimes brought with them young historians or
economists anxious to meet the celebrated revolutionary.

He rarely spoke of himself or of his life, and never
about his origin. The fact that he was a Jew neither he
nor Engels ever mentions. His references to individual
Jews, particularly in his letters to Engels, are virulent
to a degree: his origin had become a personal stigma
which he was unable to avoid pointing out in others; his
denial of the importance of racial categories, his emphasis
upon the international character of the proletariat,
takes on a peculiar sharpness of tone, directed as it is
against misconceptions of which he himself was a
conspicuous victim. His impatience and irritability
increased with old age, and he took care to avoid the
society of men who bored him or disagreed with his
views. He became more and more difficult in his
personal relations; he broke off all connexion with
one of his oldest friends, the poet Freiligrath, after his
patriotic odes in 1870; he deliberately insulted his
devoted adherent Kugelmann to whom some of his
most interesting letters were written, because the latter
insisted on joining him in Karlsbad after he had made
it clear that he wished for no company. On the other
hand, when he was tactfully approached, his behaviour
could be friendly and even gracious, particularly to the
young revolutionaries and radical journalists who came
to London in growing numbers to pay homage to the
two old men. Such pilgrims were agreeably received

at his house, and through them he established contacts with his followers in countries with which he had had no previous relations, notably with Russia, where a vigorous and well-disciplined revolutionary movement had at last taken root. His economic writings, and in particular *Das Kapital*, had had a greater success in Russia than in any other country: the censorship— ironically enough—permitted its publication on the ground that 'although the book has a pronounced socialist tendency . . . it is not written in a popular style . . . and is unlikely to find many readers among the general public'. The reviews of it in the Russian press were more favourable and more intelligent than any others, a fact which surprised and pleased him, and did much to change his contemptuous attitude to 'the Russian clodhoppers' into admiration for the new generation of austere and fearless revolutionaries whom his own writings had done so much to educate.

The history of Marxism in Russia is unlike its history in any other country. Whereas in Germany and in France, unlike other forms of positivism and materialism, it was primarily a proletarian movement, marking a sharp revulsion of feeling against the ineffectiveness of the liberal idealism of the bourgeoisie in the first half of the century, and represented a mood of disillusionment and realism, in Russia, where the proletariat was still weak and insignificant by Western standards, not only the apostles of Marxism but the majority of its converts were middle-class intellectuals for whom it itself became a kind of romanticism, a belated form of democratic idealism. It grew during the height of the populist movement, which preached the need for personal self-identification with the people and their material needs, in order to understand them, educate them, and raise their intellectual and social level, and was thus equally directed against the reactionary anti-Western party with its mystical faith in autocracy, the Orthodox Church and the Slav genius on the one hand, and the mild agrarian liberalism of the pro-Westerners, such as Turgenev and Herzen, on the other.

This was the time when well-to-do young men in Moscow and St. Petersburg, notably the 'penitent' young noblemen and squires, ridden by social guilt, threw away career and position in order to immerse themselves in the study of the condition of peasants and factory workers, and went to live amongst them with the same noble fervour with which their fathers and grandfathers had followed Bakunin or the Decembrists. Historical and political materialism—emphasis on concrete, tangible, economic reality as the basis of social and individual life, criticism of institutions and of individual actions in terms of their relation to, and influence upon, the material welfare of the popular masses, hatred and scorn of art or life pursued for their own sake, isolated from the sufferings of the world in an ivory tower, were preached with a self-forgetful passion: 'A pair of boots is something more important than all the plays of Shakespeare', said Chernyshevsky, and expressed a general mood. In these men Marxism produced a sense of liberation from doubts and confusions, by offering for the first time a systematic exposition of the nature and laws of development of society in clear, material terms: its very flatness seemed sane and lucid after the romantic nationalism of the Slavophiles and the mystery and grandeur of Hegelian idealism. This general effect resembled the feeling induced in Marx himself after reading Feuerbach forty years before: it aroused the same sense of the finality of its solution and of the limitless possibility of action on its basis. Russia had not experienced the horrors of 1849, its development lagged far behind that of the West, its problems in the 'seventies and 'eighties in many respects resembled those which had faced the rest of Europe half a century before. The Russian radicals read the *Communist Manifesto* and the declamatory passages of *Das Kapital* with the sense of exhilaration with which men had read Rousseau in the previous century; they found much which applied exceptionally well to their own condition: nowhere was it as true as in Russia that 'in agriculture as in manufacture the capitalist transformation of the process of production signifies the martyrdom of the producer; the instrument of labour becomes the means of subjugating, exploiting and impoverishing the worker; the social combination and organization of the labour process functions as an elaborate method for crushing the worker's individual vitality, freedom and independence'. Only in Russia the method, particularly after the liberation of the serfs had enormously enlarged the labour market, was not elaborate, but simple.

To his own surprise, Marx found that the nation against which he had written and spoken for thirty years provided him with the most fearless and intelligent of his disciples. He welcomed them in his home in London, and entered into a regular correspondence with Danielson, his translator, and Sieber, one of the ablest of Russian economists. Marx's analyses were largely concerned with industrial societies; Russia was an agrarian state and any attempt at direct application of a doctrine

designed for one set of conditions to another was bound
to lead to errors in theory and practice. Letters reached
him from Danielson in Russia, and from the exiles
Lavrov and Vera Zassulich, begging him to apply himself to the specific problems presented by the peculiar
organization of the Russian peasants into primitive
communes, holding land in common, and in particular
to state his view on propositions derived from Herzen
and Bakunin and widely accepted by Russian radicals,
which asserted that a direct transition was possible from
such primitive communes to developed communism,
without the necessity of passing through the intermediate stage of industrialism and urbanization, as had
happened in the West. Marx, who had previously
treated this hypothesis with contempt as emanating
from sentimental Slavophile idealization of the peasants
disguised as radicalism combined with the childish
belief that it was 'possible to cheat the dialectic by an
audacious leap, to avoid the natural stages of evolution
or shuffle them out of the world by decrees', was by now
sufficiently impressed by the intelligence, seriousness,
and, above all, the fanatical and devoted socialism of the
new generation of Russian revolutionaries to re-examine
the issue. In order to do this he began to learn Russian;
at the end of six months he had mastered it sufficiently
to read scientific works and confidential government
reports which his friends succeeded in smuggling to
London. Engels viewed this new alliance with some
distaste: he had an incurable aversion to everything
east of the Elbe, and he suspected Marx of inventing
a new occupation, in order to conceal from himself
his reluctance, due to sheer physical weariness, to
completing the writing of *Das Kapital*. After duly

tunnelling his way through an immense mass of statistical and historical material, Marx wrote two lengthy letters in which he made considerable doctrinal concessions. He admitted that if a revolution in Russia should be the signal of a common rising of the entire European proletariat, it was conceivable, and even likely that communism in Russia could be based directly upon the semi-feudal communal ownership of land by the village as it existed at the time; but this could not occur if capitalism continued among its nearest neighbours, since this would inevitably force Russia in sheer economic self-defence along the path already traversed by the more advanced countries of the West.

The Russians were not alone, however, in paying homage to the London exiles. Young leaders of the new united German social democratic party, Bebel, Bernstein, Kautsky, visited him and consulted him on all important issues. His two eldest daughters had married French socialists and kept him in touch with Latin countries. The founder of French social democracy, Jules Guesde, submitted the programme of his party to him, and had it drastically revised. Marxism began to oust Bakuninist anarchism in Italy and Switzerland. Encouraging reports came from the United States. The best news of all came from Germany, where the socialist vote, in spite of Bismarck's anti-socialist laws, was mounting with prodigious speed. The only major European country which continued to stand aloof, virtually impervious to his teaching, was that in which he himself lived and of which he spoke as his second home. 'In England', he wrote, 'prolonged prosperity has demoralized the workers . . . the ultimate aim of this most bourgeois of lands would seem to be the establishment of a bourgeois aristocracy and a bourgeois proletariat side by side with the bourgeoisie . . . the revolutionary energy of the British workers has oozed away . . . it will take long before they can shake off their bourgeois infection . . . they totally lack the mettle of the old Chartists.' He had no intimate English friends, and his relations with such sympathizers as Beesly or Belfort Bax had never been more than formal. He did indeed, in the last years of his life, allow himself to be wooed for a brief period by H. M. Hyndman, the founder of the Social Democratic Federation, who did much to popularize Marxism in England. Hyndman was an agreeable, easy-going, expansive individual, a genuine radical by temperament, an amusing and effective speaker, and a lively writer on political and economic subjects. A light-hearted amateur himself, he enjoyed meeting and talking to men of genius, and, being somewhat indiscriminate in his taste, presently abandoned Mazzini for Marx. He thus described him in his memoirs: 'The first impression of Marx as I saw him was that of a powerful, shaggy, untamed old man, ready, not to say eager, to enter into conflict, and rather suspicious himself of immediate attack; yet his greeting of us was cordial. . . . When speaking with fierce indignation of the policy of the Liberal Party, especially in regard to Ireland, the old warrior's brows wrinkled, the broad, strong nose and face were obviously moved by passion, and he poured out a stream of vigorous denunciation which displayed alike the heat of his temperament, and the marvellous command he possessed over our language. The contrast between his manner and utterance when thus deeply stirred by anger, and his attitude when giving his views on the economic events of the period, was very marked. He turned from the role of prophet and violent denunciator to that of the calm philosopher without any apparent effort, and I felt that many a long year might pass before I ceased to be a student in the presence of a master.'

Hyndman's sincerity, his *naïveté*, his affable and disarming manner, and above all his whole-hearted and uncritical admiration for Marx, whom, with typical ineptitude, he called 'the Aristotle of the nineteenth century', caused the latter to treat him for some years with marked friendliness and indulgence. The inevitable breach occurred over Hyndman's book, *England for All*, which is still one of the best popular accounts of Marxism in English. The debt to Marx was not acknowledged by name, a fact which Hyndman lamely tried to explain on the ground that 'the English don't like being taught by foreigners, and your name is so much detested here. . . .' This was sufficient. Marx held violent opinions on plagiarism: Lassalle had been made to suffer for far less; he broke off the connexion at once and with it his last remaining link with English socialism.

His mode of life had scarcely changed at all. He rose at seven, drank several cups of black coffee, and then retired to his study where he read and wrote until two in the afternoon. After hurrying through his meal he worked again till supper, which he ate with his family. After that he took an evening walk on Hampstead Heath, or returned to his study, where he worked until two or three in the morning. His son-in-law, Paul Lafargue, has left a description of this room:

'It was on the first floor and well lighted by a broad window looking on the park. The fireplace was opposite the window, and was flanked by bookshelves, on the top of which packets of newspapers and manuscripts were piled up to the ceiling. On one side of the window stood two tables, likewise loaded with miscellaneous papers, newspapers and books. In the middle of the room was a small plain writing-table and a windsor chair. Between this chair and one of the bookshelves was a leather-coloured sofa on which Marx would lie down and rest occasionally. On the mantelpiece were more books interspersed with cigars, boxes of matches, tobacco jars, paperweights and photographs—his daughters, his wife, Engels, Wilhelm Wolff. . . . He would never allow anyone to arrange his books and papers . . . but he could put his hand on any book or manuscript he wanted. When conversing he would often stop for a moment to show the relevant passage in a book or to find a reference. . . . He disdained appearances when arranging his books. Quarto and octavo volumes and pamphlets were placed higgledy-piggledy so far as size and shape were concerned. He had scant respect for their form or binding, the beauty of page or of printing: he would turn down the corners of pages, underline freely and pencil the margins. He did not actually annotate his books, but he could not refrain from a question mark or note of exclamation when the author went too far. Every year he re-read his note-books and underlined passages to refresh his memory . . . which was vigorous and accurate: he had trained it in accordance with Hegel's plan of memorizing verse in an unfamiliar tongue.'

Sundays he dedicated to his children: and when these grew up and married, to his grandchildren. The entire family had nicknames; his daughters were

Qui-Qui, Quo-Quo, and Tussy; his wife was Möhme;
he himself was known as the Moor or Old Nick on
account of his dark complexion and sinister appearance. His relations with his family remained easy
and affectionate. The Russian sociologist Kovalevsky
who used to visit him in his last years, was pleasantly
surprised by his urbanity. 'Marx is usually described',
he wrote many years later, 'as a gloomy and arrogant
man, who flatly rejected all bourgeois science and
culture. In reality he was a well-educated, highly
cultivated Anglo-German gentleman, a man whose
close association with Heine had developed in him a
vein of cheerful satire, and one who was full of the joy
of life, thanks to the fact that his personal position was
extremely comfortable.' This vignette of Marx as a gay
and genial host if not wholly convincing, at any rate
conveys the contrast with the early years in Soho. His
chief pleasures were reading and walking. He was
fond of poetry and knew long passages of Dante,
Aeschylus and Shakespeare by heart. His admiration
for Shakespeare was limitless, and the whole household
was brought up on him: he was read aloud, acted,
discussed constantly. Whatever Marx did, he did
methodically. Finding on arrival that his English was
inadequate, he set himself to improve it by making a list
of Shakespeare's turns of phrase: these he then learnt
by heart. Similarly, having learnt Russian, he read
through the works of Gogol and Pushkin, carefully
underlining the words whose meaning he did not know.
He had a sound German literary taste, acquired early
in his youth, and developed by reading and re-reading
his favourite works. To distract himself he read the
elder Dumas or Scott, or light French novels of the day;

Balzac he admired prodigiously: he looked upon him as having provided in his novels the acutest analysis of the bourgeois society of his day; many of his characters did not, he declared, come to full maturity until after the death of their creator, in the 'sixties and 'seventies. He had intended to write a study of Balzac as a social analyst, but never began it. (In view of the quality of the only extant piece of literary criticism from his pen, that of Eugène Sue in the *German Ideology*, the loss may not be one to mourn.) His taste in literature, for all his love of reading, was, on the whole, undistinguished and commonplace. There is nothing to indicate that he liked either painting or music; all was extruded by his passion for books.

He had always read enormously, but towards the end of his life his appetite increased to a degree at which it interfered with his creative work. In his last ten years he began to acquire completely new languages, such as Russian and Turkish, with the ostensible purpose of studying agrarian conditions in those countries: as an old Urquhartite he laid his hopes on the Turkish peasantry which he expected to become a disruptive, democratizing force in the Near East. As his bibliomania grew, Engels's worst fears became confirmed; he wrote less and less, and more crabbedly and obscurely. The second and third volumes of *Das Kapital*, edited by Engels, and the supplementary studies which formed the fourth volume, edited by Kautsky from posthumous material, are greatly inferior in mental power, lucidity and vigour to the first volume which has become a classic.

Physically he was declining fast. In 1881 Jenny Marx died of cancer after a long and painful illness. Each had come to conceive life impossible without the other. 'With her the Moor has died too', Engels said to his daughter Eleanor. Marx lived for two more years, still carrying on an extensive correspondence with Italians, Spaniards, Russians, but his strength was virtually spent. In 1882, after a particularly severe winter, his doctor sent him to Algiers to recuperate. He arrived with acute pleurisy which he had caught on the journey. He spent a month in Northern Africa which was uncommonly cold and wet, and returned to Europe ill and exhausted. After some weeks of vain wandering from town to town on the French Riviera in search of the sun, he went to Paris, where he stayed for a time with his eldest daughter Jenny Longuet. Not long after his return to London, news came of her sudden death. He never recovered from this blow, and hardly wished to do so: he fell ill in the following year, developed an abscess in the lung, and on 14 March 1883 died in his sleep, seated in an armchair in his study. He was buried in Highgate cemetery and laid next to his wife. There were not many present: members of his family, a few personal friends, and workers' representatives from several lands. A dignified and moving funeral address was delivered by Engels, who spoke of his achievements and his character:

'His mission in life was to contribute in one way or another to the overthrow of capitalist society . . . to contribute to the liberation of the present-day proletariat which he was the first to make conscious of its own position and its needs, of the conditions under which it could win its freedom. Fighting was his element. And he fought with a passion, a tenacity and a success which few could rival . . . and consequently was the best-hated

and most calumniated man of his time . . . he died, be-
loved, revered and mourned by millions of revolutionary
fellow workers from the mines of Siberia to the coasts of
California, in all points of Europe and America . . . his
name and his work will endure through the ages.'

His death passed largely unnoticed among the general
public; *The Times* did, indeed, print a brief and in-
accurate obituary notice, but this, although he died
in London, appeared as a message from its Paris correspondent who reported what he had read in the French
Socialist Press. His fame increased steadily after his
death as the revolutionary effects of his teaching became
more and more apparent. As an individual he never
captured the imagination either of the public or of
professional biographers to such an extent as his more
sensitive and more romantic contemporaries; and
indeed Carlyle and Herzen were infinitely more tragic
figures, tormented by intellectual and moral conflicts
which Marx neither experienced nor understood, and far
more profoundly affected by the *malaise* of their generation. They have left a bitter and minute account of it,
better written and more vivid than anything to be found
in Marx or in Engels. Marx fought against the mean
and cynical society of his time, which seemed to him to
vulgarize and degrade every human relationship, with
a hatred no less profound. But his mind was made of
stronger and cruder texture; he was insensitive, self-
confident, and strong willed; the causes of his unhappiness lay wholly outside him, being poverty, sickness, and
the triumph of the enemy. His inner life was tranquil,
uncomplicated and secure. He saw the world in simple
terms of black and white; those who were not with him
were against him. He knew upon whose side he was,

his life was spent in fighting for it, he knew that it would ultimately win. Such crises of faith as occurred in the lives of the gentler spirits among his friends, the painful self-examination of such men as Hess or Heine, received from him no sympathy. He looked upon them as so many signs of bourgeois degeneracy which took the form of morbid attention to private emotional states, or still worse, the exploitation of social unrest for some personal or artistic end—frivolity and self-indulgence criminal in men before whose eyes the greatest battle in human history was being fought. This uncompromising sternness towards personal feeling and almost religious insistence on a self-sacrificing discipline, was inherited by his successors, and imitated by his enemies in every land. It distinguishes his true descendants among followers and adversaries alike from tolerant liberalism in every sphere.

Others before him had preached a war between classes, but it was he who conceived and successfully put into practice a plan designed to achieve the political organization of a class fighting solely for its interests as a class— and in so doing transformed the entire character of political parties and political warfare. Yet in his own eyes, and in those of his contemporaries, he appeared as first and foremost a theoretical economist. The classical premisses on which his economic doctrines rest are to-day largely superseded; contemporary discussion proceeds upon a different basis. The doctrine which has survived and grown, and which has had a greater and more lasting influence both on opinion and on action than any other view put forward in modern times, is his theory of the evolution and structure of capitalist society, of which he nowhere gave a detailed exposition. This theory, by asserting that the most important question to be asked with regard to any phenomenon is concerned with the relation which it bears to the economic structure, that is the balance of economic power in the social whole of which it is an expression, has created new tools of criticism and research whose use has altered the direction and emphasis of the social sciences in our generation.

All those whose work rests on social observation are necessarily affected. Not only the conflicting classes and their leaders in every country, but historians and sociologists, psychologists and political scientists, critics and creative artists, so far as they try to analyse the changing quality of the life of their society, owe the form of their ideas in part to the work of Karl Marx. More than half a century has passed since its completion, and during those years it has received more than its due share of praise and blame. Exaggeration and over-simple application of its main principles have done much to obscure its meaning, and many blunders, both of theory and of practice, have been committed in its name. Nevertheless its effect was, and continues to be, revolutionary.

It set out to refute the proposition that ideas govern the course of history, but the very extent of its own influence on human affairs has weakened the force of its thesis. For in altering the hitherto prevailing view of the relation of the individual to his environment and to his fellows, it has palpably altered that relation itself; and in consequence remains the most powerful among the intellectual forces which are to-day permanently transforming the ways in which men think and act.

BIBLIOGRAPHY

I. ORIGINAL WORKS

THE complete edition of the works and private papers of Marx and Engels is still unfinished: their publication in the original languages which was commenced in Berlin under the auspices of the Marx-Engels-Lenin Institute was interrupted by Hitler's accession to power in 1933. The Russian translation simultaneously and subsequently published by the Institute in Moscow has considerably outstripped the German edition, and is almost but not quite complete (1947). The best-known works have been made accessible to English readers by a series of competent translations published by Messrs. Martin Lawrence (now Lawrence and Wishart). It includes, up to date: *The German Ideology* (Pts. I and III), *The Poverty of Philosophy*; *The Communist Manifesto*; *Wage, Labour and Capital*; *The Class Struggles in France*; *The Eighteenth Brumaire of Louis Bonaparte*; *Civil War in France*; *Civil War in the United States* and *Revolution in Spain* (collections of Marx's newspaper articles, letters, documents, &c.); *Correspondence, 1846–1895* (a large and well-edited selection of letters by Marx and Engels); *Letters to Dr. Kugelmann,* and the *Critique of the Gotha Programme*; of works by Engels: *Germany: Revolution and Counter-revolution*; *Ludwig Feuerbach and the Outcome of Classical German Philosophy*; *Socialism: Utopian and Scientific*; *Herr Eugen Dühring's Revolution in Science*; *Dialectics of Nature*; *The British Labour Movement*; and several other works. The best English translation of the first volume of *Capital* is by E. and C. Paul (Everyman's Library: Dent), the only available English version of Vols. II and III is still that by E. Untermann (Chicago: C. H. Kerr & Co.); Vol. IV (*Theories of Surplus Value*) has not been translated into English. There are also versions of *A Contribution to Political Economy* (trans. N. I. Stone: C. H. Kerr & Co.); *Value, Price and Profit* (ed. by E. M. Aveling, Allen and Unwin) and *Letters on India* (ed. by B. P. L. and F. Bedi, Lahore: Contemp. India Publications). Two useful compendia, which include a good many of the works cited above, are: *A Handbook to Marxism* (ed. E. Burns: Gollancz) and *Selected Works* (2 vols., Lawrence and Wishart).

II. BIOGRAPHIES

The standard work is *Karl Marx* by Franz Mehring, brought up to date and excellently annotated by E. Fuchs and translated by E. Fitzgerald. *Karl Marx: a Study in Fanaticism*, by E. H. Carr, is a lively and interesting book based on detailed original research, which, on points of fact, supersedes all previous authorities. An equally scrupulous work but more sympathetic to its subject and his teaching is *Karl Marx: Man and Fighter*, by B. Nicolaievsky and O. Maenchen-Helfen, which also embodies original material, particularly from Russian sources. Biographies exist also by John Spargo and Otto Rühle, and shorter lives by M. Beer, R. W. Postgate and C. J. S. Sprigge; the last of these contains many points of interest. The standard biography of Engels is by G. Mayer (abridged and translated by G. and H. Highet, ed. by R. H. S. Crossman).

III. CRITICAL STUDIES

Of the immense polemical literature which surrounds Marx and Marxism the following works, of those written in or translated into English, are likely to be of most interest to the general reader: *Karl Marx and the Close of his System*, by E. v. Böhm-Bawerk (this, and the works by H. W. B. Joseph and V. Simkhovich cited below, constitute the most formidable attacks upon Marx's economic doctrines). A counter-attack is provided by R. Hilfferding's *Böhm-Bawerk's Criticism of Marx*. *What Marx Really Meant*, by G. D. H Cole, the most competent large-scale popular exposition of Marxism, if not of Marx's own views, since Engels and Hyndman. *Towards the Understanding of Karl Marx* and *From Hegel to Marx*, by S. Hook, lucid and penetrating critical studies of Marx and his predecessors. *The Labour Theory of Value in Karl Marx*, by H. W. B. Joseph, *Marxism versus Socialism*, by V. Simkhovich (for both these, see above). *The Open Society and its Enemies*, by Dr. Karl Popper: a work of exceptional originality and power. The second volume provides the most scrupulous and formidable criticism of the philosophical and historical doctrines of Marxism by any living writer. Alexander Gray in *The Socialist Tradition*, a model of clear, at times brilliant, always entertaining, exposition. This provides a very intelligent if more personal and less detailed examination of Marxism. *Karl Marx*, by Karl Korsch, a learned but ponderously written examination of Marxism in his historical setting. *Historical Materialism and the Economics of Karl Marx*, by Benedetto Croce, an essay of arresting originality. *The Marxist Philosophy and the Sciences*, by J. B. S. Haldane, a stimulating, if not wholly convincing, discussion of the usefulness of the method of dialectical materialism in the natural sciences, based largely on the theories of Engels. *Marxism, Is it Science?* by Max Eastman, an essay of characteristic brilliance by this sharp and original critic and excellent writer, bitterly condemned as a heretic by orthodox Communists. *Darwin, Marx, Wagner*, by Jacques Barzun, a very readable essay. *To the Finland Station*, by Edmund Wilson (New York, 1940) contains a very striking intellectual portrait of Marx. *What is Marxism?* by Emile Burns, an orthodox Communist account. *An Essay on Marxian Economics*, by Joan Robinson, a characteristically penetrating study. S. H. Chang, *The Marxian Theory of the State* (Philadelphia, 1931), a painstaking treatise. *Karl Marx in his Earlier Writings*, by H. P. Adams, a competent summary of the writings before the 'London' period. M. M. Bober's *Karl Marx's Interpretation of History* (U.S.A., 1927), a dry but useful study of this topic. A short but exceptionally able study of historical materialism by J. L. Gray forms a chapter of *Social and Political Thinkers of the Nineteenth Century*, ed. F. J. C. Hearnshaw. The pages devoted to Marxism in *A History of Political Theory*, by G. H. Sabine, an excellent summary. *The Economic Doctrines of Karl Marx*, by K. Kautsky, the classical exposition of Marxist economics. *Karl Marx*, by H. J. Laski, the best short summary of Marx's achievement. The same author's *Communism* in this series is, despite its shortness, so far as is known to the writer, the best analysis of the movement and its intellectual basis in any language. *Karl Marx's Capital*, by A. D. Lindsay, an exceptionally fair discussion of its subject. *Marx, Engels, Marxism*, by N. Lenin, a magisterial exposition and, with his *State and Revolution*.

one of the texts on which orthodox Communism is to-day based. *Essays in the History of Materialism* and *Fundamental Problems of Marxism*, by G. Plekhanov, classical treatises by the acutest thinker and most brilliant writer among the immediate successors of Marx and Engels. A duller but solider work is *Karl Marx and Friedrich Engels*, by D. B. Ryazanov, the most erudite of all Marxists, and the most pedestrian. *The Theory and Practice of Communism*, by R. N. Carew-Hunt (London, 1950), and *What is Communism?*, by J. P. Plamenatz (London, 1947), should also be consulted.

INDEX

GALAXY BOOKS *for the Discriminating Reader*